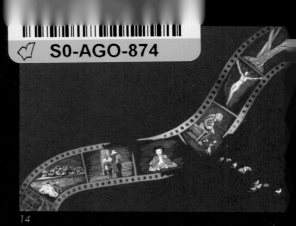

13

14

15

16

17

18

19

20

21

23

SEEROON YERETZIAN

ABRIL Publishing
Glendale, California
2011

This book is dedicated to my late husband,
Haroutioun Aram Yeretzian

Copyright © 2011 Seeroon Yeretzian
Art Direction by Harry Mesrobian / Gemini Designs
Printed in USA by Color Depot, Glendale, California

Published in the United States by ABRIL Publishing
415 E. Broadway, Suite 102, Glendale, California 91205
Telephone (818) 243-4112 Facsimile (818) 243-4158
Email: noor@abrilbooks.com   Website: www.abrilbooks.com

Library of Congress Control Number: 2011915712

ISBN 978-0-9796842-7-2

Visit the official website of Seeroon Yeretzian at: www.seeroonart.com

Cover
SELF PORTRAIT 1993
oil on canvas
28 × 22 in. 71.12 × 55.88 cm.

Dedication page
HAROUT YERETZIAN II 1983
oil on canvas
28 × 28 in. 71.12 × 71.12 cm.

Foreword page
POMEGRANATE OFFERING 2008
oil on canvas
22 × 28 in. 55.88 × 71.12 cm.
Lora Kuyumjian

End page
FRAMED BY LOVE 2009
oil on cotton liner
50 × 37 in. 127 × 93.98 cm.
Seeroon standing next to Self Portrait, 2010

Back cover
THIS IS WHAT THE WORLD WOULD LOOK LIKE WITHOUT ART (FRAME NOT INCLUDED) 2007
oil on canvas
36 × 48 in. 91.44 × 121.92 cm.

CONTENTS

FOREWORD

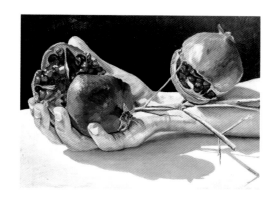

I first met Seeroon Yeretzian at the world famous Abril Bookstore in 1986. That same year I began my apprenticeship under her husband, Harout Yeretzian, who was one of the store's proprietors. This was no ordinary bookstore; it was more akin to an academy for the arts. At any given time, it was not unusual to rub elbows with prominent visiting writers, musicians and artists. Little did I know then that this small and cramped bookstore, which also doubled as a print shop, would set an indelible mark on my life and reward me with two life-long friendships.

Quiet, modest, and a comforting presence - that's the way I remember Seeroon then, and that's the way I would describe her today. Fate would have it that she and I work alongside and I unequivocally can state two things about her; first and foremost is that she is an exceptional woman with a generous nature and kind soul, and second is that you will never find her sitting idle. Her artistic maturity and creative prowess is a direct result of her faithful dedication to keeping an open mind, remaining in constant motion and being productive.

Seeroon's art style is elusive to categorize, yet distinct and unmistakable. Her work reflects upon her life experience. Although they express her point of view, they are no different in terms of value from those that we all share as human beings - seeking answers to the meaning of life. Her father was a survivor of the Armenian Genocide. She was born into the new generation of hope, growing up in the refugee camps of Lebanon, witnessing its civil wars, and ultimately finding passage to the land of new hope in America. Look closely at her work and you will clearly identify her search for personal identity, whether it be on a human level or in paying homage to her Armenian heritage.

This art book is a collection of works that span over thirty years and serve as testament to Seeroon Yeretzian as an artist. At long last, we the viewing public, have been given a gift in the form of a book that encapsulates her talent.

On a personal note, I would like to thank Seeroon for her invaluable friendship and congratulate her on the publication of this book. May the fruits of your labor of love be in abundance. I wish you continued success.

HARRY MESROBIAN

SEEROON YERETZIAN

DR. GARABED BELIAN

A versatile artist, with diverse talents, working in oils, acrylics and gouache, her works are images drawn from her heritage, history, myth and legend, where she fully explores the mysteries of her subconscious mind. These images often have a plurality of meaning and her work reveals her sense of humor with so many illusionistic inconsistencies and a contrasting logic, that it can be often interpreted as an unpleasant dream.

Seeroon interprets her dreams, concerns, ambitions and aspirations, as well as all her emotions, in a poetic content. Thus, she captures the poetry of dreams rendering them in figurative and narrative form, often with the randomness of fantasy. She believes in an enchanted inner vision and her subject matter comprises allegories of life and death.

The artist manipulates the pictorial elements in her work to intensify psychological content and favors forms based on the imagery of the unrestrained subconscious.

1. MADONNA IV 1994
mixed media on paper 24 × 18 in. 60.96 × 45.72 cm.
Sylvia Minassian

2. BELLE LAIDE 1994
oil on paper 32 × 20 in. 81.28 × 50.8 cm.
Edmond Azadian

1

While she expresses her thoughts and emotions in dream-like images, her work indicates that she believes art should be based on sensory experiences rather than on lifeless imitations of visual reality.

Seeroon's art defies all categorization as she is involved in many modern movements. Often her work has an emotional intensity that ranges from deep melancholy to painful discordance to a kind of ecstatically restorative jubilation, extending from shrieking figures, disturbed and emotionally charged images, to more serene depictions of decorative and colorful representations of the illuminated ornate initials of the Armenian Alphabet.

Seeroon has the ability to use long-established traditions with freshness, individuality and intelligence. Some of her images, such as "Day and Night" 1994, recall medieval works of art with an elaborate and complicated iconography - similar to her Madonnas. These formal creations are open to multiple interpretations leading to the symbolic unexplained machinations of fate, where her violation and distortion of the human figure reflects the destruction and torture found in our society.

Seeroon is interested not in capturing reality, but in the presentation of visual metaphors. The male figure in "Eternity" 1990, exhibits his superhuman strength acting as a cross to a helpless figure as if crucified unto his body, essentially a modern variant to crucifixion; a baroque allegory.

Similarly in "Veni, Vidi," "Transposed," "C'est La Vie," all of 1994, the artist combines different images in her composition, recalling Robert Rauschenberg, an important Proto-Pop artist, except that unlike Rauschenberg, most of her images are related and dissolve into logical relationships. The crucified figure, dangling feet, prostrate forms, all are not only put together with wit and charm, but create shock and surprise. The overall effect creates a reality that dwells deep within the human spirit where the effect could be shocking and even devastating.

Seeroon's subjects can be gay or gloomy. Her figures are lost in a luminous mist, web-like barriers or partially covered by organic and plant elements, yet they retain a humanized rhythm with a sympathetic unity binding together figures, movement and feeling.

2

3. COMPENSATION 1990
acrylic on canvas 18 × 18 in. 45.72 × 45.72 cm.
Hovsep and Hilda Fidanian

The faceless figures denote loss of identity, stressing inner states, inner tensions and sensations irrespective of external forms. Her work demonstrates a fascination with metaphysical symbolism, expressed in a witty and visually seductive manner. She depicts her Madonnas like other images as a metaphor for passionate human emotions, human suffering, social injustice.

The artist has altered her subject matter and experimented with different themes throughout her artistic career, reflecting her emotional climate dominating her vision at any given time.

Many of Seeroon's paintings recapitulate themes she must have long been obsessed with, such as the precarious existence of her ancestors throughout the ages. A representative example is "The Echo" 1983. Three faces with mask-like quality and elongated necks, create a strangely intense and morbid physical quality. The surface textures are luminous and wrinkled and even tortured in character. These three human specimens who are so ruthlessly revealed in her work are ravaged by physical exhaustion and have exceeded the limits of human endurance.

"The Echo," emotionally compelling, is painted with great vigor. Here, she resorts to an alarming liberation of gesture and directness of stroke; although respecting the general outline of her characters, she has omitted all detail.

The influence of Edvard Munch and the German Expressionists is evident where she emphasizes heightened emotion and stress, pathos, violence, suffering and rage, portrayed by the artist's subjective vision.

Even more emotionally compelling is the dramatic painting, "The Warlord" 1985, where Seeroon depicts dying humans, decapitated heads and mounds of

3

human heads. "The Chorus" 1987, portrays the silent and unheeded shriek of different expressions. In these works, as in the "Expressions" 1982, and other similar compositions, Seeroon portrays symbolic representations of Genocide, murder and human injustice. Here, the ravages of decay and death are depicted with horrifying intensity.

Seeroon's diverse artistic talents include graphic design and illustrations. She has produced the most popular Armenian poster in existence, "The Splendor of Aypupen" 1989, a masterpiece which gave her great reputation. Similar to this is the "Latin Alphabet" 1992, composed of stylized letters made up of mythical creatures, angels, flower parts, animals, reptiles, birds and sea-monsters. Each letter is a complete representation by itself.

4. *Renowned art collector Richard Manoogian*
next to "Beautiful Aypupen" 1996

5. ANGEL OF THE CENTURY 2001
Seeroon's statue on display in Century Plaza Towers,
Century City, California, as part of the Los Angeles city
"Community of Angels" art project

6. HISTORY ON THE MOVE 1999
mixed media on paper 30 × 22 in. 76.2 × 58.88 cm.
Edmond Azadian

4

5

The art of Seeroon Yeretzian is broad in concept, style and thematic variety. As an artist she remains an intriguing creator of psychologically arresting, poetically evocative images.

In her dream narratives we find variable experimentation, daring brush strokes and striking color combinations where, using free association, dreams and imagination, myth and legend as tools for total freedom and expression, she creates paintings which are vital and explosive, having ambiguous images of emerging and receding moods, expressed in diverse art styles. Using as a vehicle the tragic history of her ancestors, pivotal personal experiences in her life, the joys and sorrows of mankind, she recreates her world of dreams and captures the poetry behind emotions.

In "The Academy" 1985, she is uncertain as to where her own head will land upon the pile of other artists' heads.

6

COMPASSIONATE EXPRESSIONISM

SAHAG TOUTJIAN

At the first glance upon entering the exhibition hall, your senses are stirred with perplexity. You advance. You pass in front of the canvases. At first indistinctly, then more clearly, your self-assurance begins to falter. Your thoughts refuse to take refuge in their deceptive initial tranquility. The accepted formulations on art become rather irrelevant and superfluous. Here we are dealing with the real world: rough, brute and merciless. Here, also, we are dealing with a specific art of painting that arcs itself over the world, with love and compassion, to portray it with a genuine expression of feelings and experience.

First and foremost, one is impressed with the audacity Seeroon Yeretzian displays in the selection of themes and the diversity of aesthetic experimentation. She scrutinizes, she probes, and she questions hardened "realities." She explores personal, novel parallels of depth and form. She tries to speak entirely new idioms of the artistic language – albeit maintaining creative authenticity and truthfulness.

With her, this simple aesthetic fact is once more confirmed: the common denominator of all authentic artistic creation, regardless of the different modes of style and expression, is the distinctly individual expressive innovation, or, to use a popular term, an inimitable self-stamped "signature." This means that it is possible to accomplish genuine artistic formulation of the self same given reality in both figurative and abstract execution.

7

8

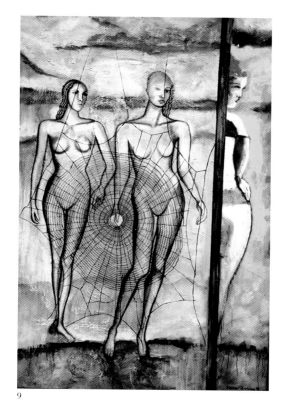

9

The stylizations of painterly expression are numerous and diverse. It is possible to communicate in the limited "tongue" of duplication or replication, more or less reminiscent of photography. It is possible to offer the essence of appearances in sharp abstraction. But it is also possible – as in Seeroon Yeretzian's case – to lead the process of abstraction not to its supreme or utmost level, but only to the point necessary for expressive forcefulness, while at the same time maintaining a meaningful communion and immediate interaction with the outside world. Both of these two components are equally important for best appreciating her art. On the one hand, certain stylistic leverages of abstract art assist immensely in her expressive consummation. On the other hand, her communion with the real world helps her express in a dynamic intimation truths that are commonly deprived of their civil rights.

Seeroon Yeretzian's works display a responsible and healthy stance toward unhealthy human and public situations. The injustice, ugliness and deformities of social life are her themes – and the object of her "silent" indignation. Her canvasses tend to be artistic constructs hoisted against them.

The theme of "women's rights" is the most immediate motivating force of her creative efforts. But this leads her not to feminist repudiation, but to the inclusive attitude of humanism. In numerous works this horrible social condition is underlined – both woman's and man's concurrent exploitation and crucifixion, the inequality of them both, which is a result of the same prevalent inhumane conditions. She raises this issue through all the palettes she employs in her canvases. The crucified woman, her helpless male mate, relegated to the background in his muscular absurdity, the two other females or "thieves" crucified on the flanks – or, in another instance, the two children who animate the frontal plan – all join together on the modernized symbolic cross.

The second important theme dominating the canvases is human suffering and deprivation; man's humiliation by man and man's inhumanity towards man. Here, manifested are the Armenian Genocide on the one side, and the American homeless on the other.

The works dedicated to the Armenian Genocide are expressions of profound tragedy; powerful emotions. These clay skulls have been brought to

10

13

11

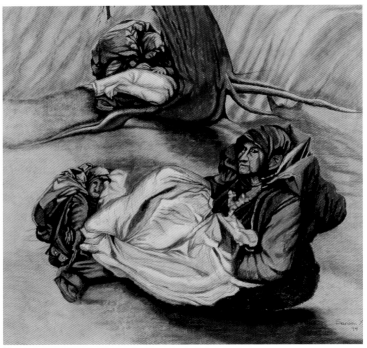

12

the canvas with such infinite tenderness! Bodiless heads. Headless bodies. Otherworldly faces, hollowed eyes and bones. The canvas frame is unable to contain so much inhumanity – so that within the picture a special frame is provided, wherefrom overflow the torrents of tragedy, with the heaviness of dark blue, the eruptions of scorching red, the outburst of a sad green reminiscent of death rather than life. In another part of the canvas, the contents of the inner frame and the space outside it dissolve into each other to become one.

In numerous works, the bleak, shameful themes of the homeless tower up like an immense question mark against the sneaking self-alienation of American democracy. The series of contorted canvasses depicting an old woman dragging life's vanity, turned into an unbearable leaden burden, along cold sidewalk pavements, is a pointed indictment of this modern grotesque fiction called civilization. (With bitter irony, the old, old phrase "to grow old gracefully" comes to mind.) Rough and deadly are the cobblestones where the figure of a youth or the blunt juxtaposition of the lively colors of two exquisite dolls is spread like a lifeless gray lump of flesh. This depravity is a betrayal of man's rationality against man. "Home, Sweet Home" 1983, is an inscription under the extremely poignant, shocking image of a desperate homeless person.

In the string of themes brought to the canvas, prominent importance has been allocated to social vices: deceit (masks, masks, masks), the social humiliation of women, the enervating claws of a deceptive civilization (and the annihilation of refreshing childlike spontaneity by the tie-clad gray establishment), Armenian and non-Armenian contemporary scenes, the all-pervading melancholy and

13. NUDE FEMALE NO. 21 1982
charcoal on paper 18 × 24 in. 45.72 × 60.96 cm.

14. NUDE FEMALE NO. 7 1982
charcoal on paper 24 × 18 in. 60.96 × 45.72 cm.

15. NUDE FEMALE NO. 25 1982
pastel on paper 23 × 18 in. 58.42 × 45.72 cm.

13

the wingless hope hardly stirring at times, and finally, the oblique solace of-fered by the creative passion of art.

At the focus of Seeroon Yeretzian's oil paintings, one often finds the fiery trin-ity of red-orange-yellow, whose tense dynamism is counterbalanced by the thick black of the background. Besides this, the occasional white renders the theme more salient, as with the white faces of the three women which are contrasted to the neon colors wrapping their up-for-sale bodies. On a second plane one notices the hues of rust and especially an unwholesome green which so aptly imparts meaning to the given moment. A gray or black gloom, which expresses the dark tragedy in leaden hues, comes to further enhance the impressions. Brown, gray and black are commonly dominant in the case of acrylics. These, however, are at times mellowed down by the light white of the background, and in some in-stances, blaze up with the glitter of gay shards of rainbow colors.

The harmonious symbiosis of colors and hues find their culmination in the gouaches. In this connection, it is worth to note the ornamental letters of the Armenian alphabet, which invoke the authentic colors and hues of our miniature art heritage.

One should not forget the pencil and pen drawings which animate objects and situations. Seeroon Yeretzian creates under the immediate stimulation of her psyche, conceptions and fantasy. Honesty renders to her forms of ex-pression a fresh immediacy and a keen emphasis which best illuminates the inner spiritual vistas of the artist. The series of chilly masks, in eloquent yet restrained communicativeness, symbolizes her unequivocal stance against personal hypocrisy and social deceit.

One can attribute the essential aesthetic qualities of Seeroon Yeretzian's paintings to the influence of the best traditions of German expressionism — specifically, the potency of emphatic and bold black or dark lines, the em-ployment of color generally as a means to display emotional states; the pre-ponderance of heavy colors (black, brown, etc.) for expressing emotionally and authentically the harsh mercilessness of life. Her creations exhibit the keen perception of the uncertain fate of contemporary aimless man, the pro-found grasp of inner human aspirations, and the robust dynamism of un-yielding audacity of modern thinking in search of answers.

14

15

AN EXPRESSIONIST PAINTER

PROF. GEVORG KHERLOBIAN

Today we are fortunate to be able to appreciate the paintings of a representative of the contemporary Armenian expressionist school. Their author, Seeroon Yeretzian, comes across as confident in her canvases, as they are fed from both global and national springs. The masculine bodies she depicts often recall ancient Etruscan murals and pictures on ancient Greek pottery. It isn't hard to note the influence of Hieronymus Bosch, Edvard Munch and Max Beckman in her portraits.

Also, the voices of protest from Goya's "Colossus" are heard in Seeroon's canvases. Henri Rousseau's primitivism, as well as Monet's, Degas' and Matisse's color techniques make their presence felt.

Following modern art's dicta, Seeroon doesn't want to be carried away with games of light and shadow. Her canvases are composed of separate, flat color pieces, which are laid side by side. For her, the picture is more important than what it represents. The canvas lives by its own laws. Each brushstroke, each color segment and color solution is equally authentic, regardless of its basis in thought or nature. Each of her lines or colors is emphatically expressive, supersaturated with emotions, which creates a personal dynamism and movement. It is palpable that the painter has many ideas to share. The painter's penetrating eye sees that which is present on the other side of the cover or surface of modern life. She aspires to express not the surface but the interior. To achieve this, she creates her own symbols, which reveal the real inner world of man and show how feeble and helpless he is against the force of progress. Sometimes, following Seurat's practice, she aspires to surrender to the scientific imperative to create law and order,

17

and composes rigorously moderated, controlled canvasses. Emulating Van Gogh, she doesn't depict the typical but that which is particular, which is unique. She transforms the personal and unique into a means to express her emotions. She achieves these via prominent colors and daring deformations. She succeeds in making her message get across.

When they connect, Seeroon Yeretzian's canvases mostly evoke emotions and thoughts with social intensity. She tries to draw attention to yet unresolved highly important issues or newly manifested faults, the existent public evil. She demands a safer and more beautiful future for children. She defends the ignored rights of all the homeless; she declares war against all sorts of inhumanity perpetrated against man, genocide in the first place. She's a protector of women's rights; not only women's social and political rights, but of her beauty, femininity and motherhood. The crucifixion is very operative in her subconscious. In ancient times, the cross was a symbol of the sun, of light and eternity. Later, in the Roman world, it became a tool of punishment. The Christian church and faith accepted it as the symbol of man's salvation. Seeroon's cross is an original synthesis of those three symbols. Modern man is crucified, i.e., he is tortured, because he is despised. Today, man, as a generator of progress, is a source for the good, is a sun, is light and warmth. Today, man is in need of love and salvation. He's in need of a strong backing. He's in need of a support.

Seeroon Yeretzian's art aspires to make an appeal, so that those needs of man can be met. Her appeal is made in a charming language, that is presented with the help of a beautiful naturalness, in an expressionistic manner.

18

SELF PORTRAIT 1993
gouache on board 20 x 15 in. 50.8 x 38.1 cm

WHAT IS ART FOR ME

SEEROON YERETZIAN

19

20

I am a Lebanese-born Armenian. I have lived the past 35 years as an American, in the state of California, a cradle that absorbs the kaleidoscope of nationalities from around the world.

I was born in the Tiro refugee camp of Beirut, Lebanon. Rats, mice, mosquitoes, roaches, flies, and slugs were our blood brothers and constant companions. We were all natural recyclers of the city's trash.

My father Dikran, who was a musician, used to repair old and broken musical instruments, and the ones that were irreparable, he took apart and used them for various purposes in our living quarters.

My mother Berjouhi, who was a born artist unaware of her multiple talents, created beautiful ornate needle works and taught me (as she was taught): "It is dishonorable for girls to study art and paint nude figures. A girl should marry and have children."

I listened to my mother. I honorably married and had a child. However, after coming to America, I "dishonorably" studied art and pursued it as my career, and yes! - even painted nude figures.

21

19. *Seeroon as a toddler resting in a wooden box*

20. *Needlework by mother Berjouhi*

21. *Father Dikran on accordion and his band*

22. *Seeroon, father Dikran and eldest sister Dikranouhi in Tiro refugee camp*

22

23. An Armenian petroglyph from the Sisian region.

24. ARMENIAN MOTIFS 2003
gouache on board 30 × 40 in. 76.2 × 101.6 cm.

25. "TO KNOW WISDOM…" 2010
oil on canvas 48 × 36 in. 121.92 × 91.44 cm.

23

Painting has become a habit-forming drug that I am addicted to, and use, every moment of my life. My physical and emotional evolution as an artist has concentrated on several motifs, and I classify my art into two categories:

Art of My Ancestral Land

• PETROGLYPHS OF ARMENIA - The amazing images inside the caves and open air rock carvings of Armenia were done by the earliest known artists of my people. I wanted to go to our roots and bring out these age-old images (mainly the human stick figures, not the animals) to give them new expressions of dance, music, life and love.

• THE ILLUMINATED MANUSCRIPTS - the crown jewels of Armenian art from the 8th to 19th century, generally ignored by world art. Instead of copying in miniature form (as was the practice at the time before printing was invented) I work in an enlarged format and in a style that has become my own, especially the Ornate Initials which give me artistic orgasms. I have created initials that were nonexistent in the manuscripts and recreated the existing ones. Though "the painstaking art of illumination" is a giant thief that has stolen the years of the artists in the past, I have personally lived the stolen years of my life with this art.

Art Sans Frontieres

• Paintings manifested in heads and faces that are expressions of my personal, historical time and space; specifically, the "homeless," a condition of a minority turning into majority without voice.

• Paintings that are expressions of trauma that I have gone through at an early age, living in refugee camps and slums; a condition that exists everywhere, ignored by the "blind majority."

24

25

26. BEGINNING 1983
mixed media on paper 19 × 14 in. 48.26 × 35.56 cm.
Dikran and Melo Ekizian

27. TRAPPED 1996
oil on canvas 22 × 22 in. 55.88 × 55.88 cm.
Private collection

28. COMME DES GARCONNES I 1990
gouache on paper 28 × 40 in. 71.12 × 101.6 cm.
Berj and Houri Der Sahagian

26

• Paintings that deal with crucifixions of women. They are not mockeries of the Christian religion, but represent the plight of what a girl goes through from a young age to maturity in more than half of the population of the world, in so-called "advanced" societies. Instead of having scars on their palms and feet, my women images have their scars in their guts.

• Paintings that are "one with nature," combinations of nature, sea life, animals, shells, and especially women in webs; webs that we weave.

Because I am living in a time when all movements, isms, categories of art are "in," naturally, I have stepped on the ladder that was formed by all. I have all in me, and I will be compared to any, as all contemporary artists are, because the gaze of all the giant masters is always watching.

For me, painting is a process that has to be produced slowly, painstakingly, thoughtfully, and lovingly. Paintings are like children you have; they have to be different. As my mother said, "the five fingers on your hand are not the same."

The muses of my painting are ancient and new, naturalistic, photo-realistic, unstable, and changing. My daily life is turned inward and outward; a balance between ugliness and beauty with fragments of a real and surreal world. In my art, "more is more" rather than "less is more." I want to relate both art and life through the silent-static-window-stage-drama-illusion-my immortal time, the sad and happy music of my eyes.

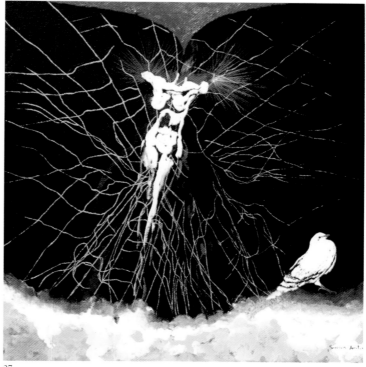

27

28

Really I do not know whether my paintings
are surrealist or not, but I do know that they
are the frankest expression of myself.

FRIDA KAHLO

1
I EXIST 2010

2
BLOOMING 1988

4

ROSE BUDS 1988

6

EVOLUTION 1998

DISPOSABLE 1982

8
EXPRESSIONS 1982

10

11
THE ECHO 1983

12
SCREAMERS 1982

13
HOMAGE TO H.B. I 1988

14
HOMAGE TO H.B. II 1988

15
HOMAGE TO H.B. III 1988

16
CONDEMNED 1988

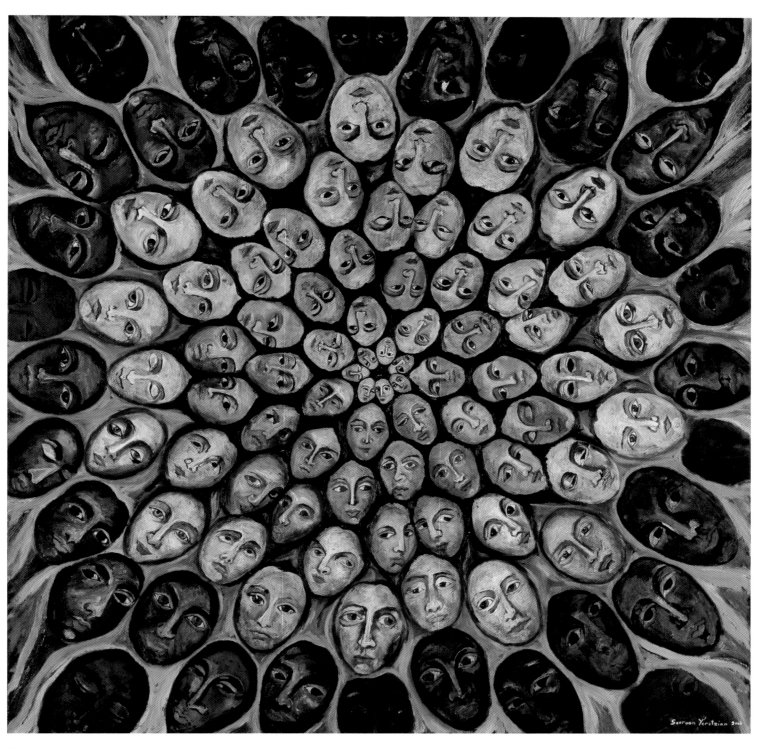

17

BLOSSOMS ERUPT 2008

18
SON OF MAN 2008

19
SONS & DAUGHTERS 2008

20
SEAGULLS 2008

21
EYES OF INFINITY 2008

22
TRINITY 2009

23
HOMAGE FROM A TO Z 2005

Whether I'm painting or not,

I have this overweening interest in humanity.

Even if I'm not working,

I'm still analyzing people.

ALICE NEEL

24
HIS HOME 1989

25
THE MATTRESS 1983

26
VANITY 1989

27
DISCARDED 1999

28
SHOWCASE V 1992

29
TIME 1999

30
TIMELESS 1999

31
THE WASTE 1989

32
THE BEGGARS 1989

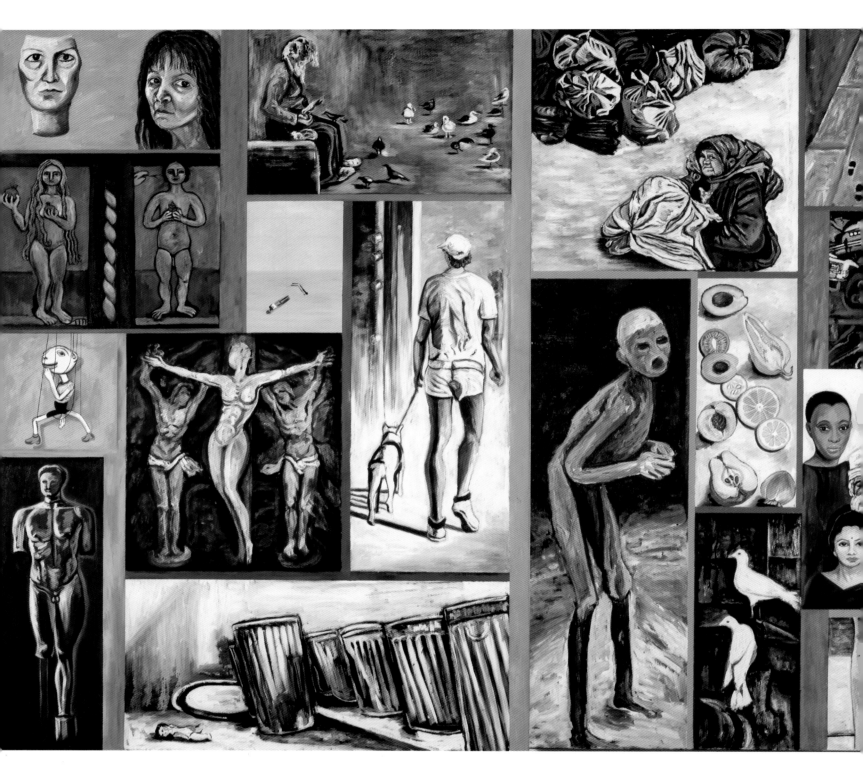

33
A DAY IN L.A. (TRIPTYCH) 1997

34
THE UNSPOKEN 1982

35
HOME SWEET HOME I 1983

36
SCRAPE 1990

37
PRAYER 1989

The object of art
is not to reproduce reality,
but to create a reality
of the same intensity.
ALBERTO GIACOMETTI

38
REMORSE 1990

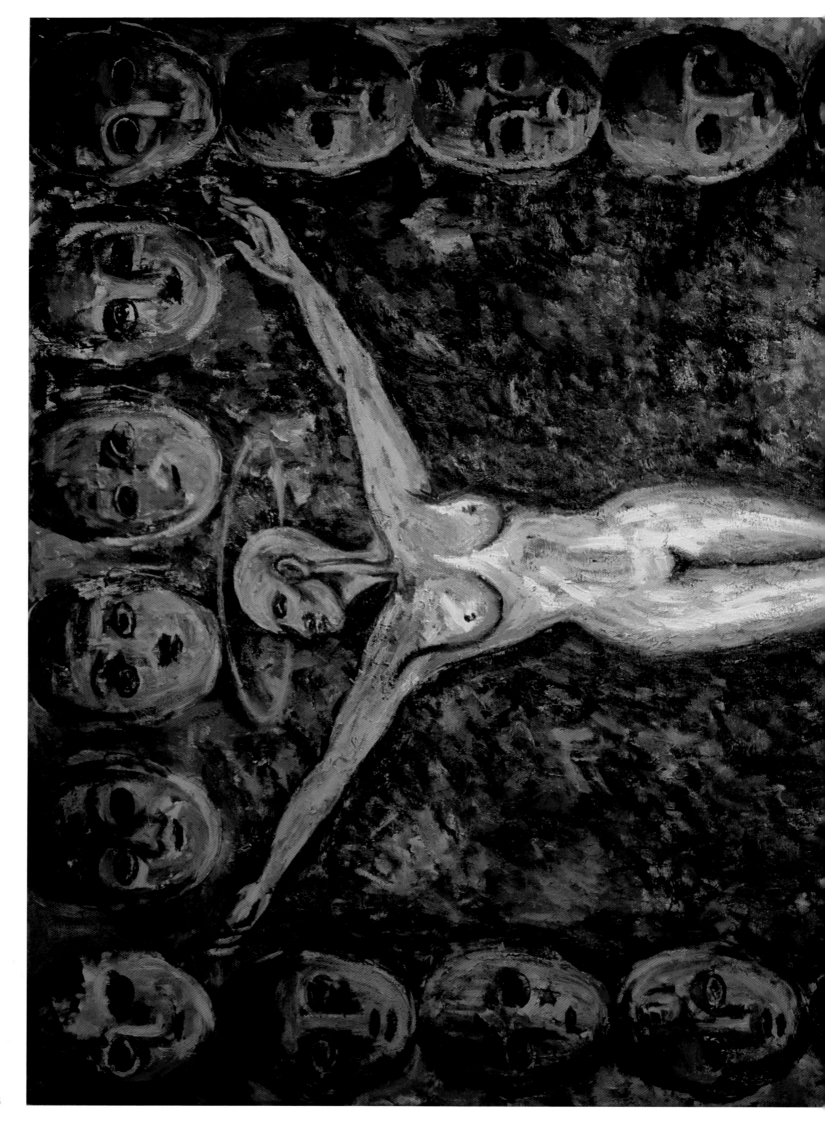

40
SOLITUDE 1992

41
A PAGE IN LIFE 1991

42

THE THREE GRACES I 1992

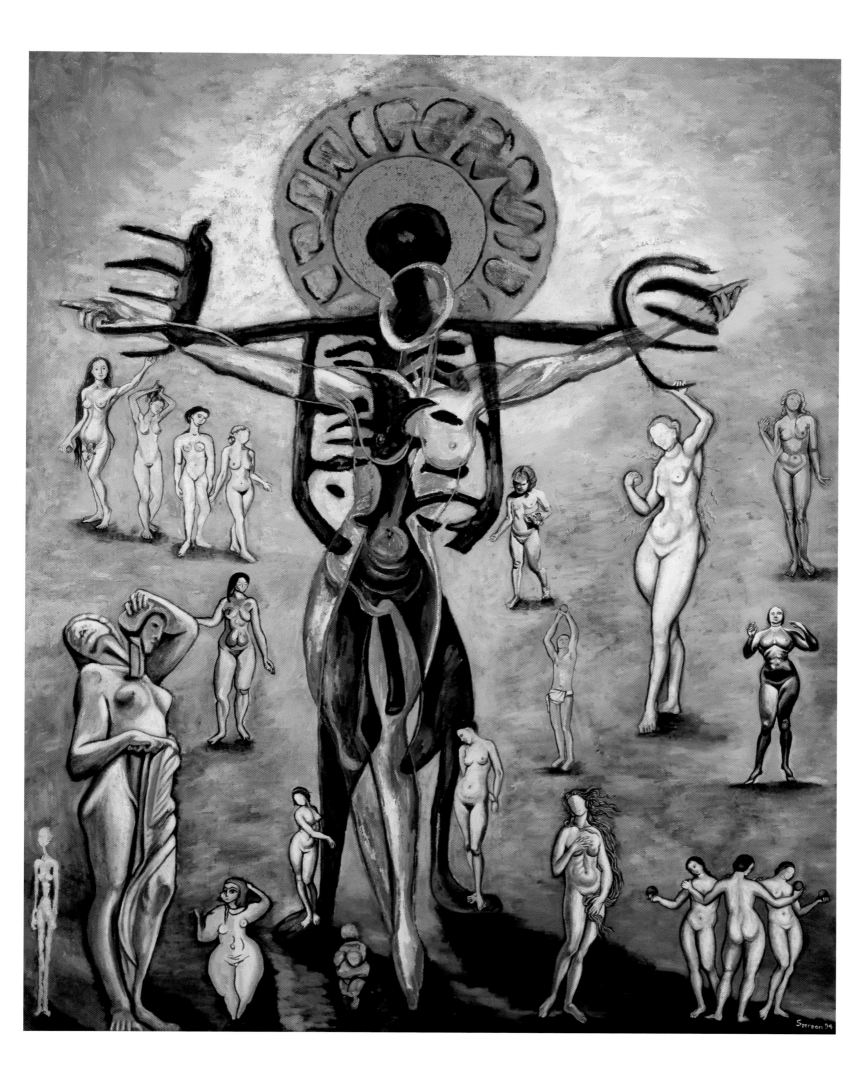

71

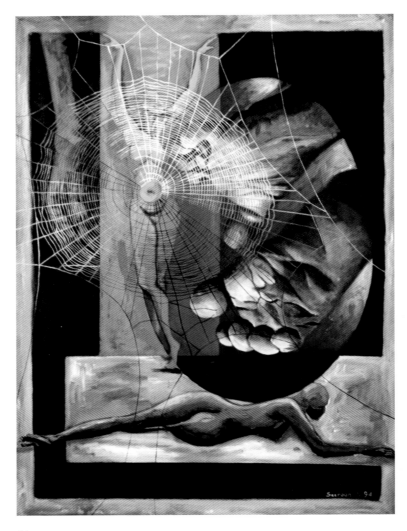

44
THE WOMB 1994

45
ADAM & EVE 1994

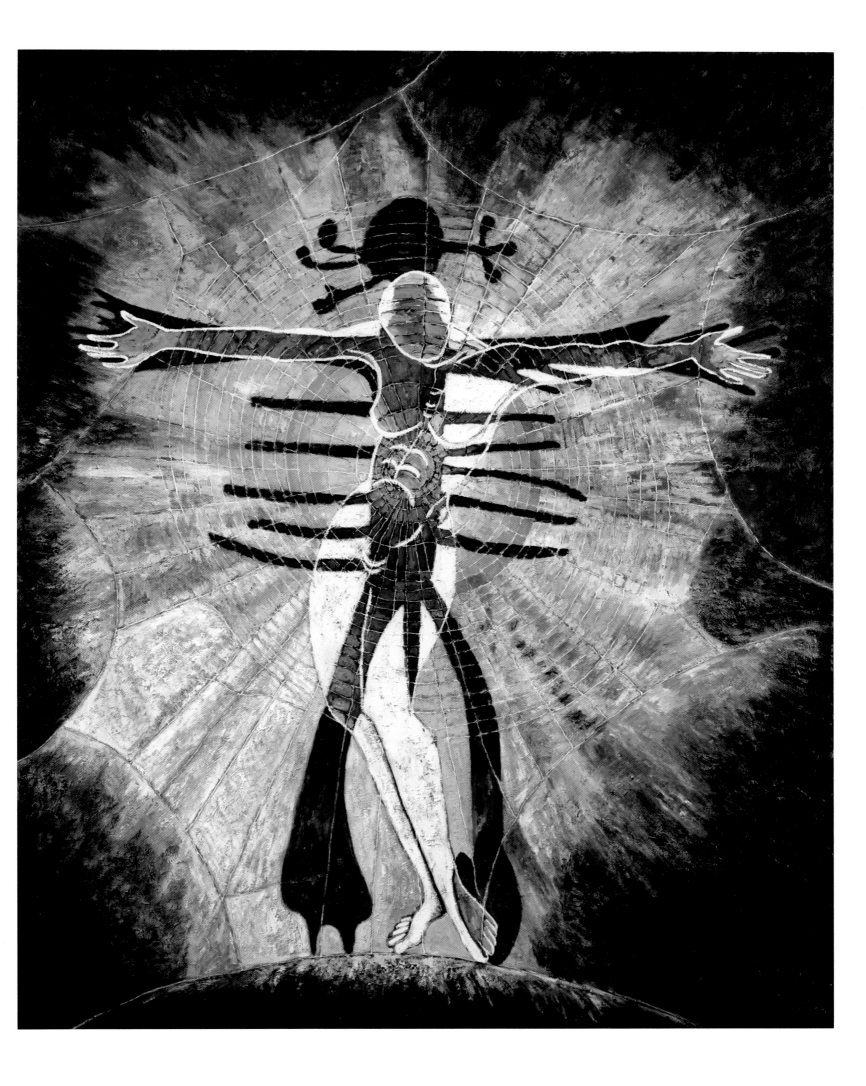

46
REFLECTION 1993

47
QUO VADIS 1994

48
TRANSPOSED 1994

49
VENI, VIDI 1994

50

ETERNITY 1990

51

FREEDOM 1993

52

FORGIVENESS 1990

53
UNCERTAINTY I 1989

54
UNCERTAINTY IV 1993

55
THE THREE GRACES II 1992

56
NATURE CRUCIFIED 2006

57

FREEDOM II 1993

58
SUBMISSION 1990

It is important to express oneself... provided the feelings are real and are taken from your own experience.
BERTHE MORISOT

59
AUTO PORTRAIT 1980-2005

60
DEATH & LIFE 1984 (DIPTYCH)

61
MY JOURNEY I 1990

Seeroon Yeretzia 09

Seeroon Y. 09

63
BEARER OF LOVE 2009

64
DAY & NIGHT 1995

65
MADONNA III 1994

66
MADONNA I 1994

67
MEDITATION 1997

68

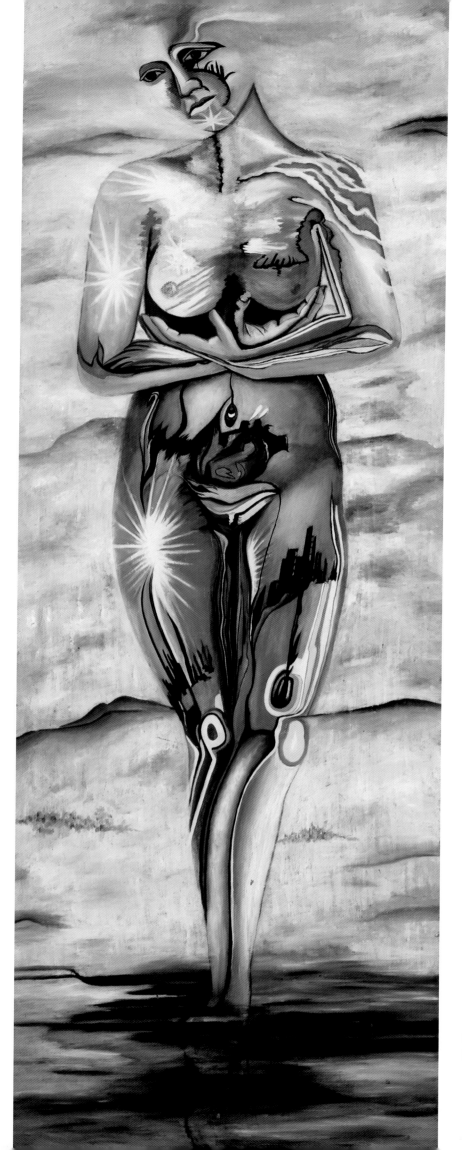

69
MOTHER EARTH 1993

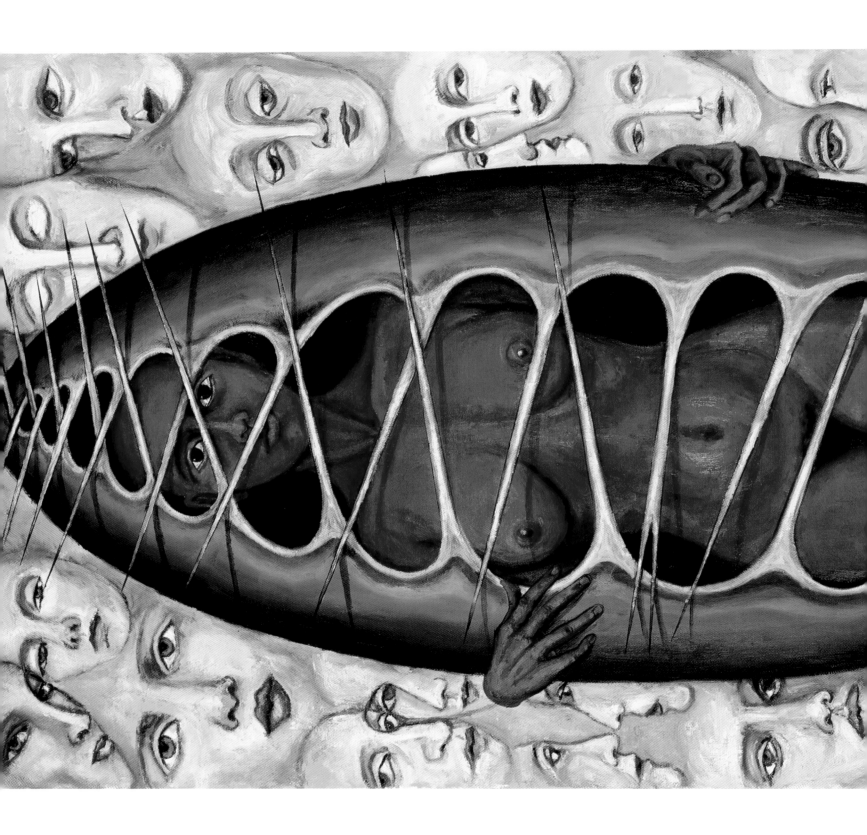

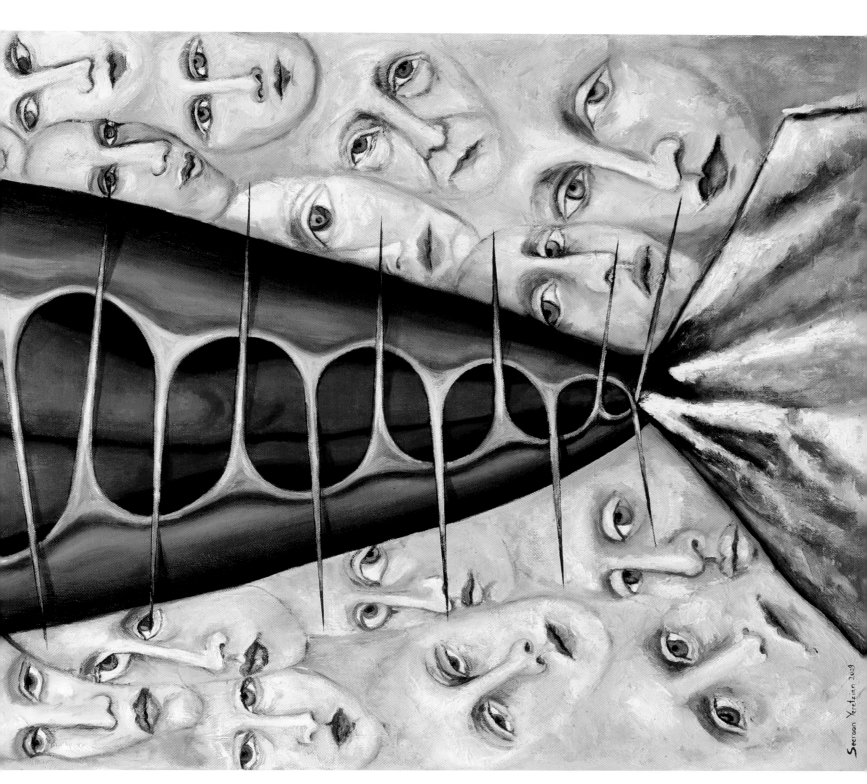

VENUS TRAPPED 2009

71

EMPTY NEST 1993

72
ENIGMA 1996

73
EVALUTION 2008

74
HUMANIMALS 2008

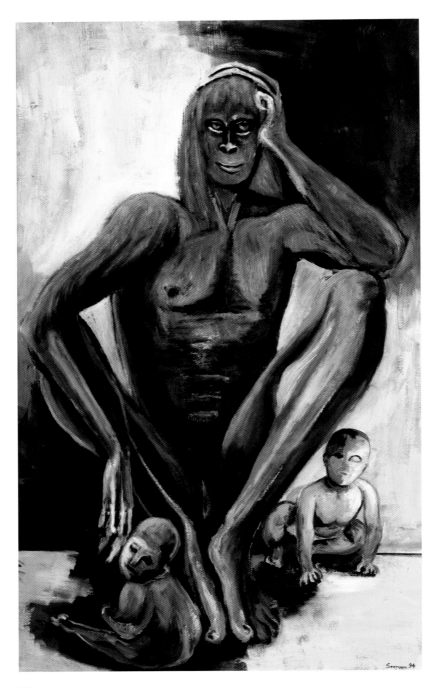

75

MONSTRE SACRE II 1994

76
INTROSPECTION 1997

The artist is a receptacle for emotions
that come from all over the place;
from the sky, from the earth,
from a scrap of paper,
from a passing shape,
from a spider's web.

PABLO PICASSO

SUPER WO-MAN 1999

78
MAN AT DAWN II 2000

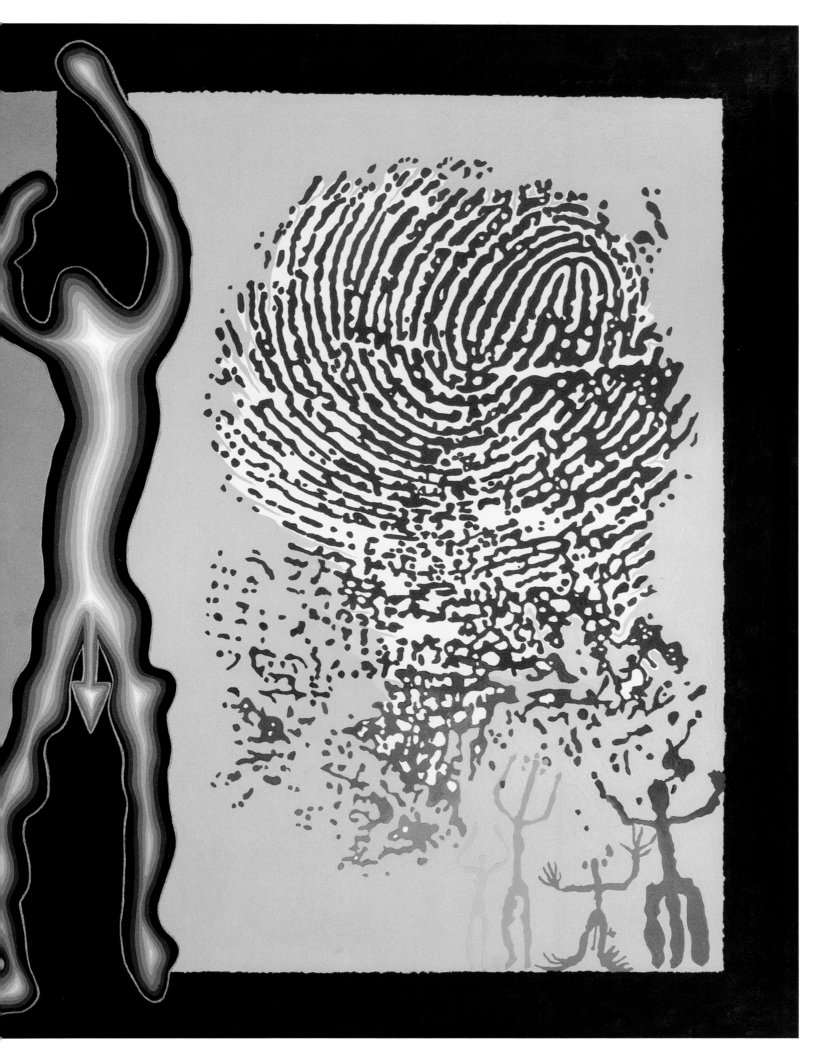

Samson Sesukail 2003

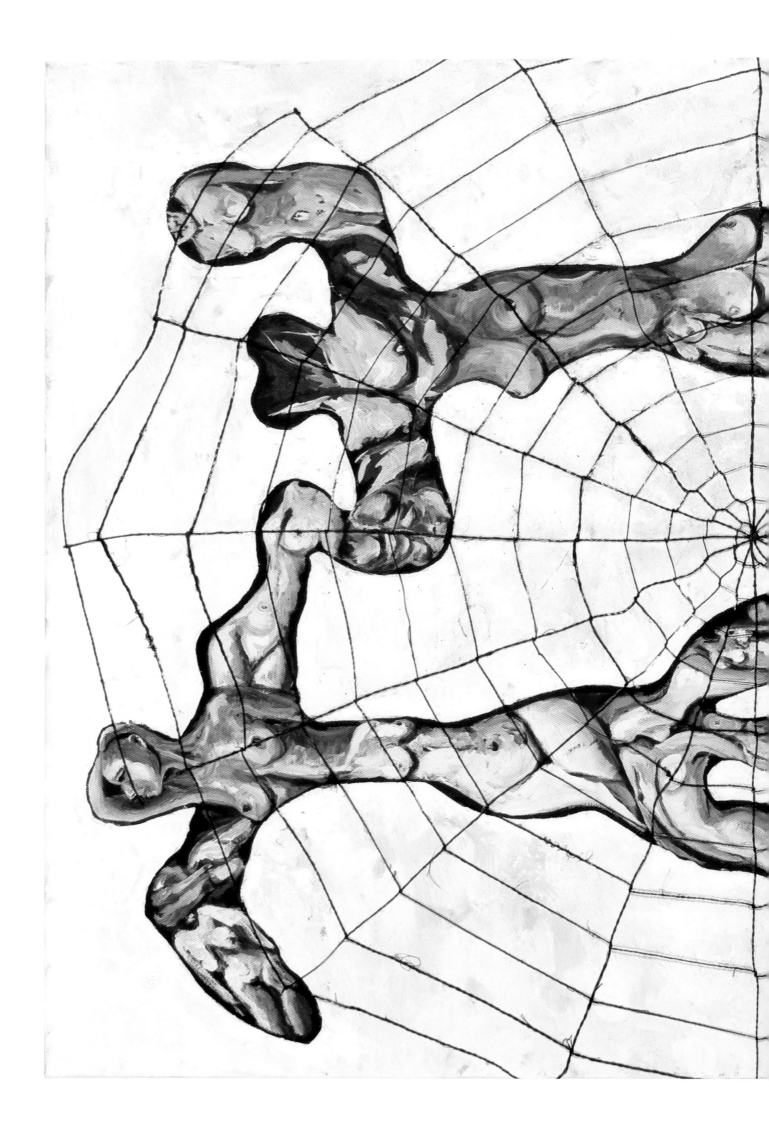

TRAPPED FOREVER 2003

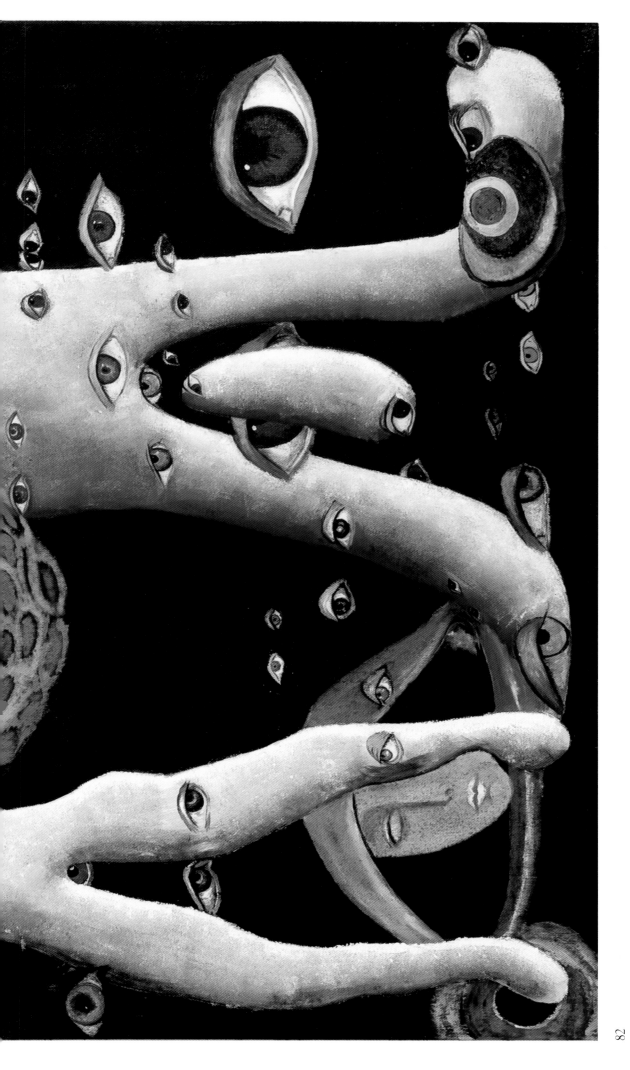

PRIMAL EYES 2003

83
HUMAN ARCHEOLOGY 2004

84

85
SANCTUARY 2004

87
HIDDEN TREASURES 2004

88

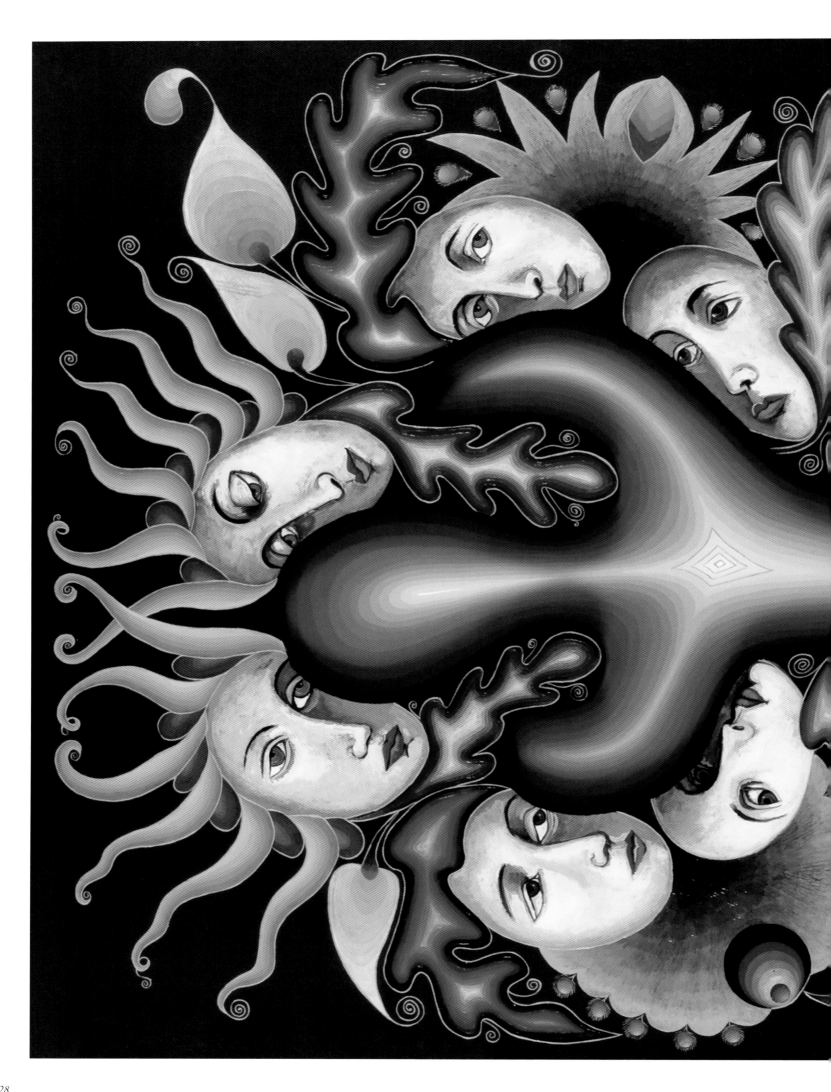

Seeroon Yeretzian
2001

90
THE OTHER SIDE 2004

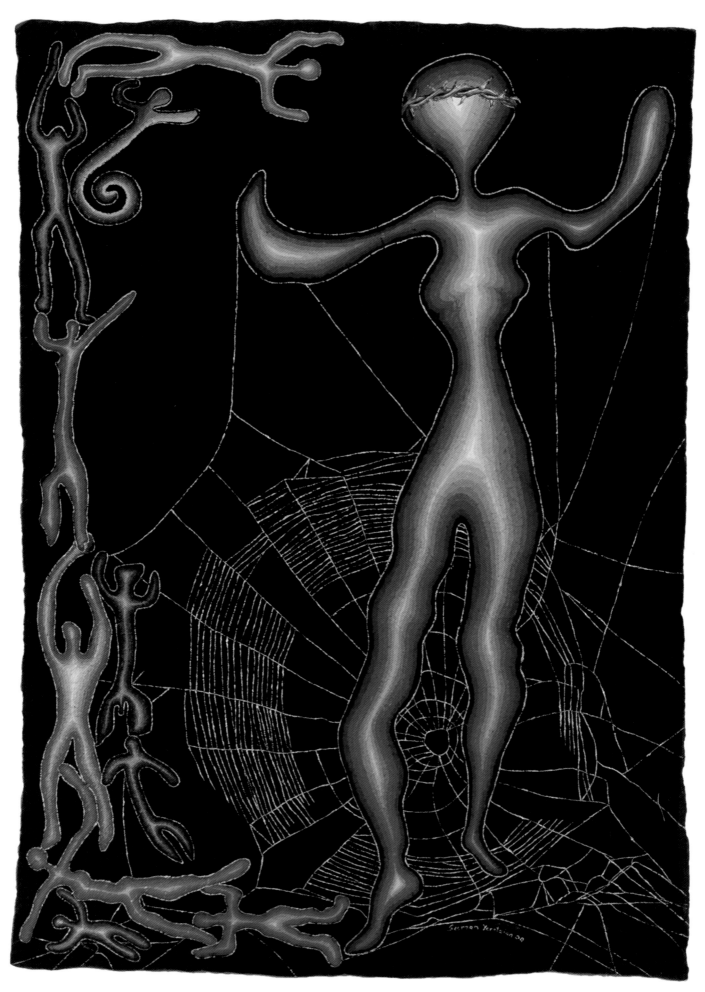

91
CROWN IN WEB 1999

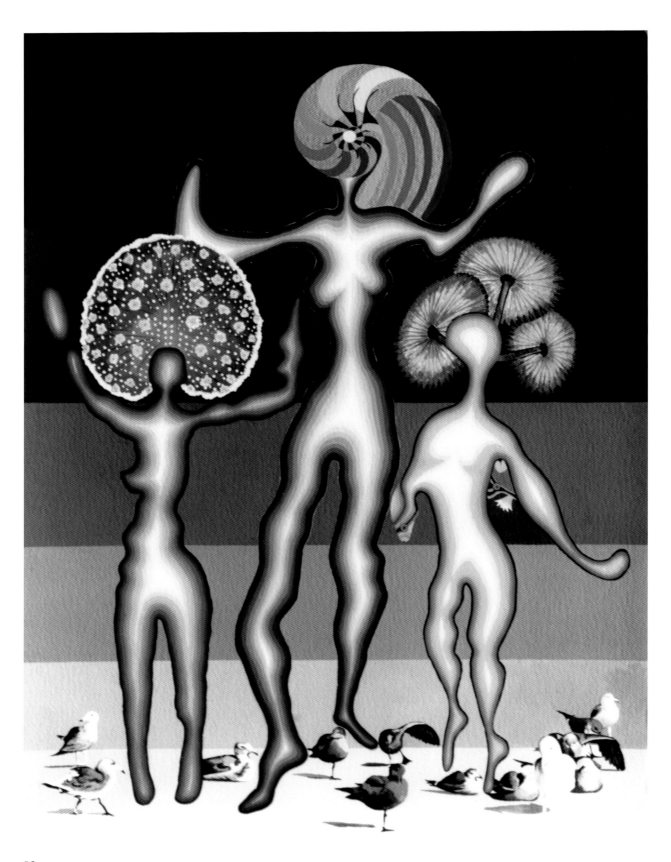

92
LAND & SEA 2000

93
HONEYCOMB I 1999

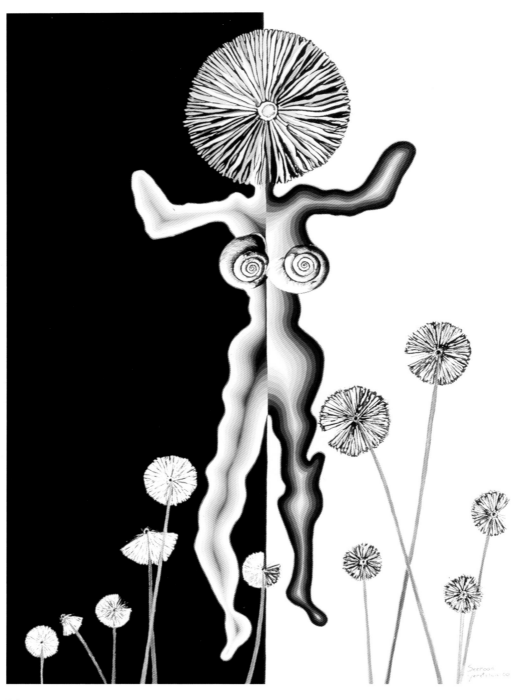

94

WISH 2000

95

GIANTS AND MIDGETS 2001

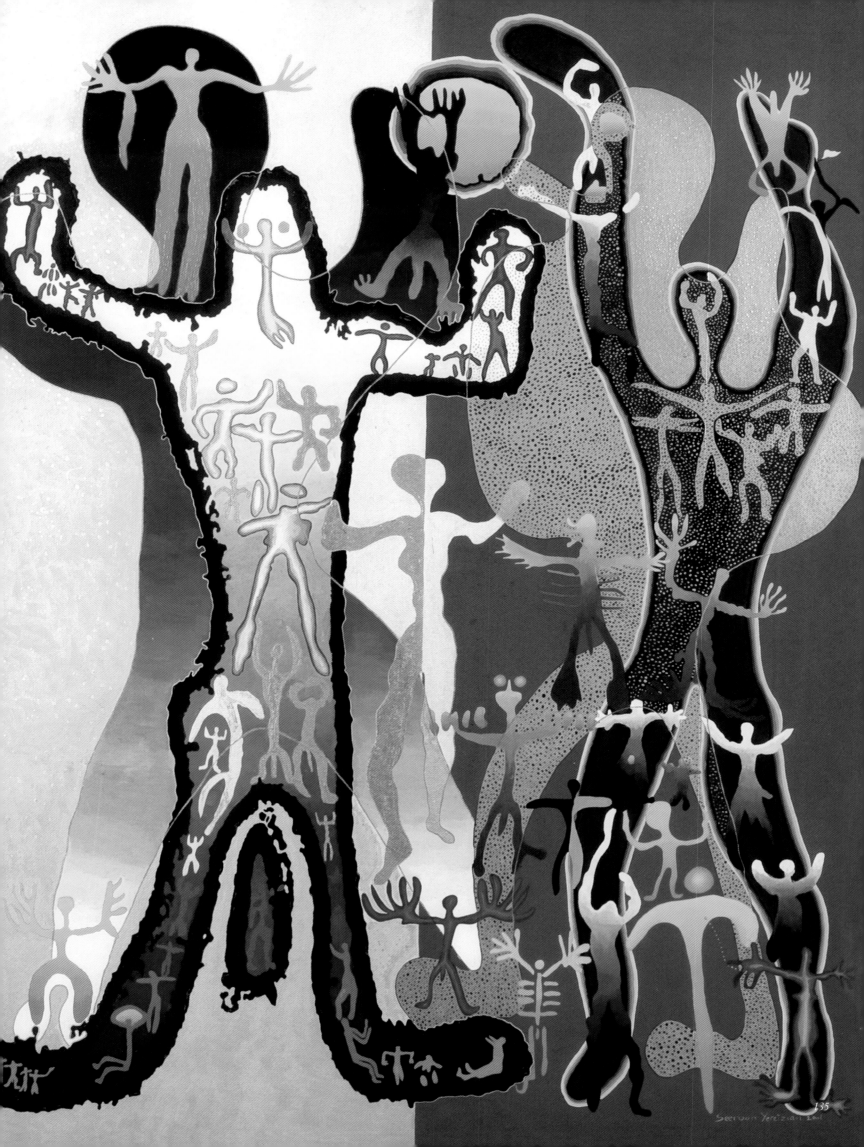

96
ECSTASY 2000

97

TRACES 1999

DANCE OF TIME 2000

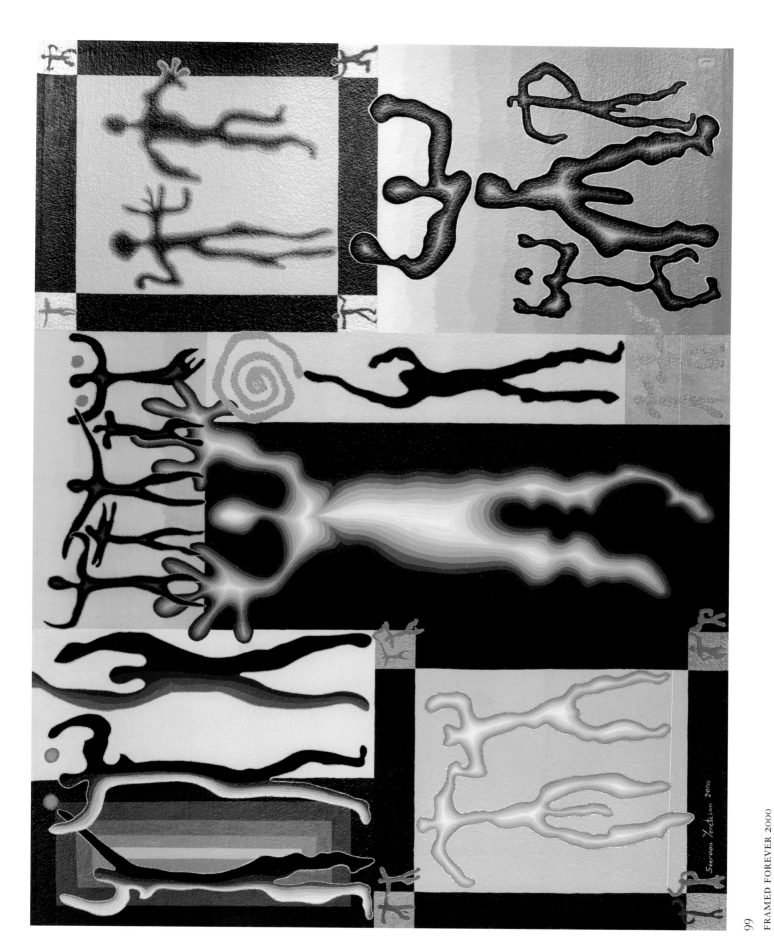

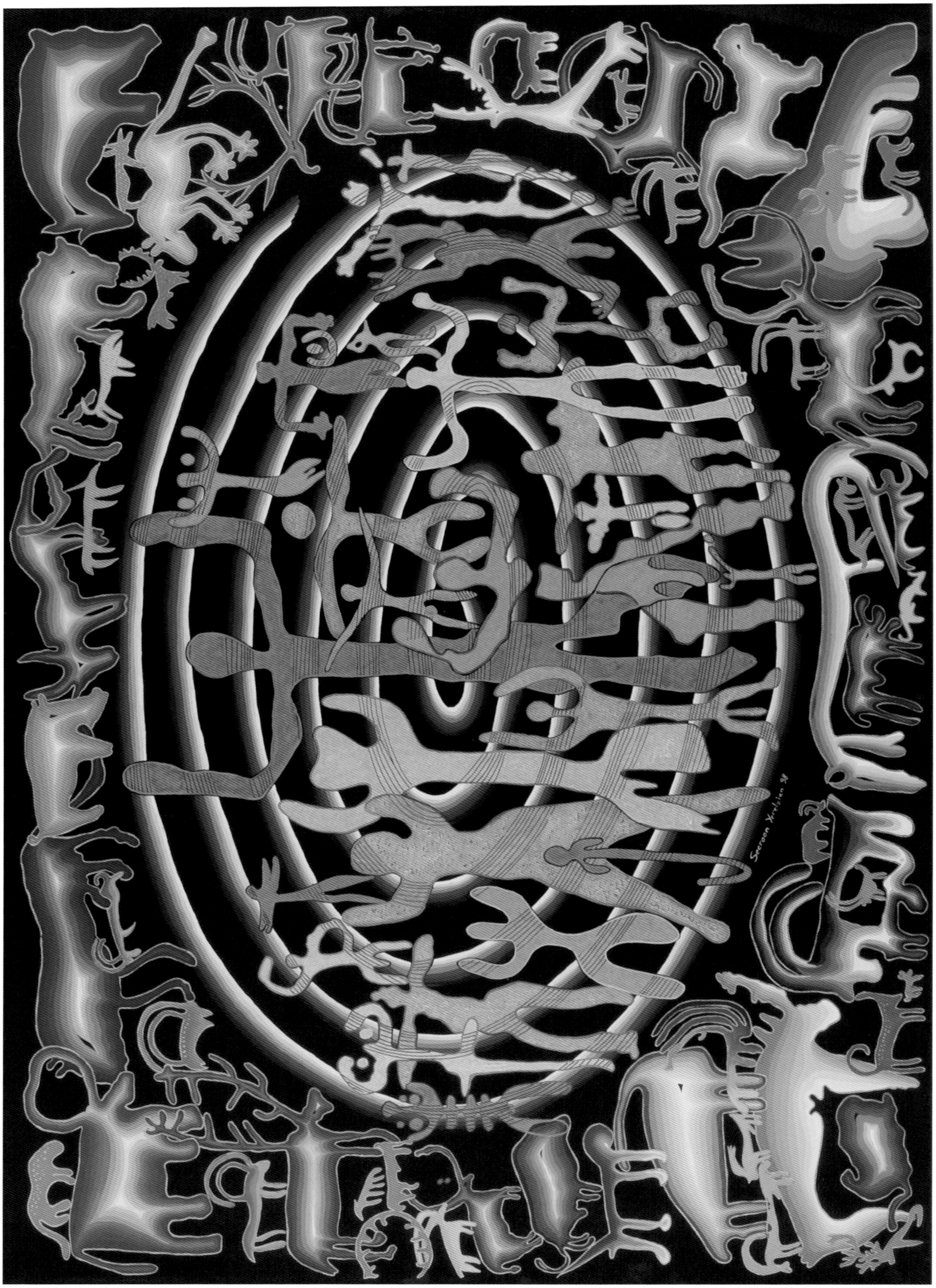

PETRIFIED CIVILIZATION 1998

140

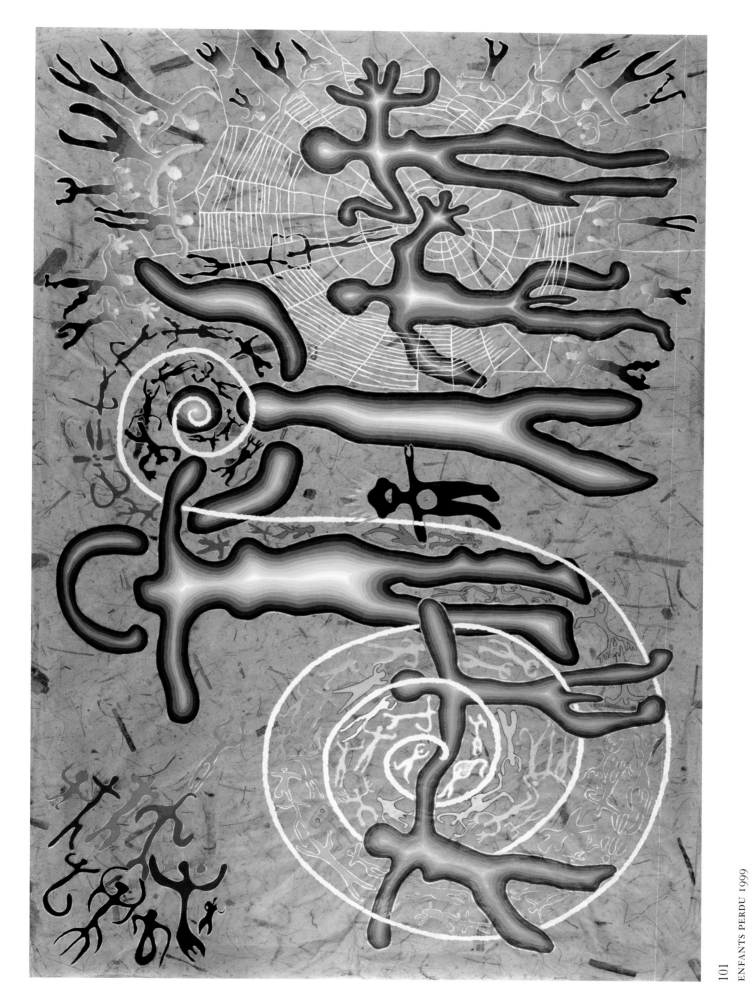

ENFANTS PERDU 1999

102
WRAPPED AROUND 2000

103

COSMIC UNITY 2000

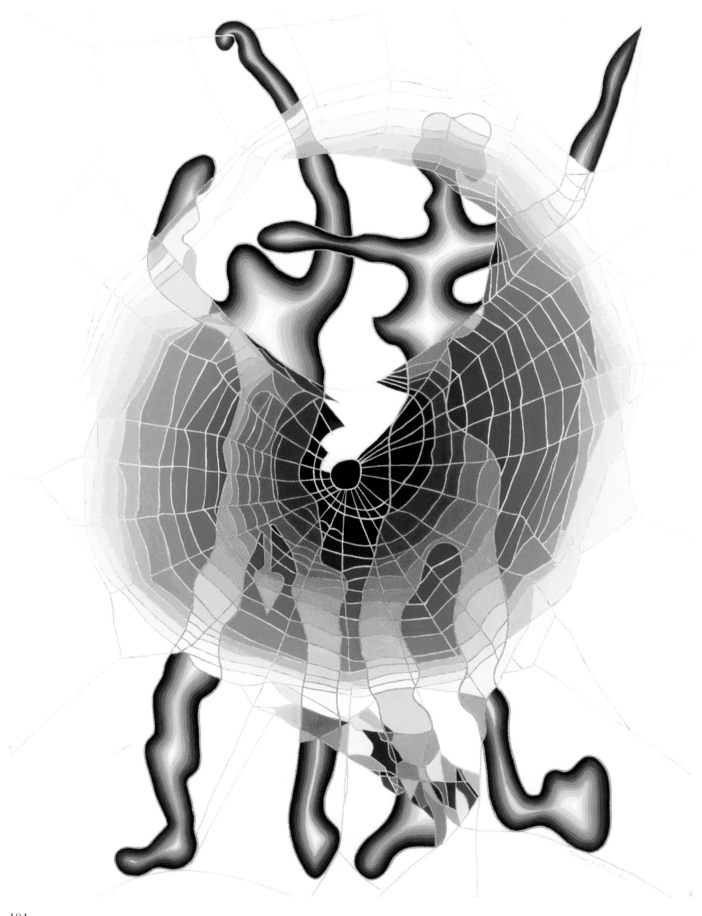

104
ENTRAPPED I 2000

105
TORNADO 1999

106
ATLAS 1999

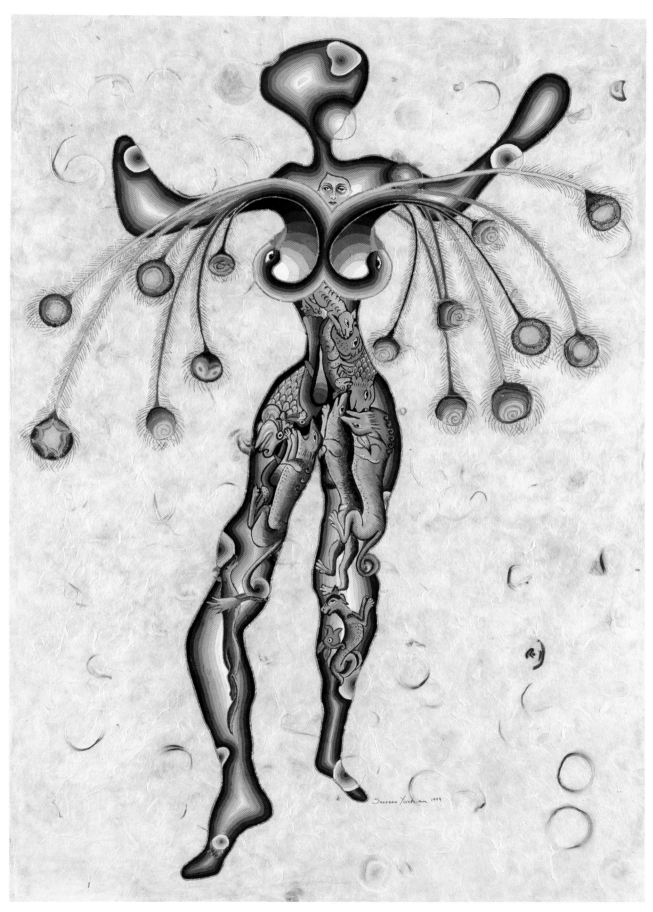

107
GODDESS 1999

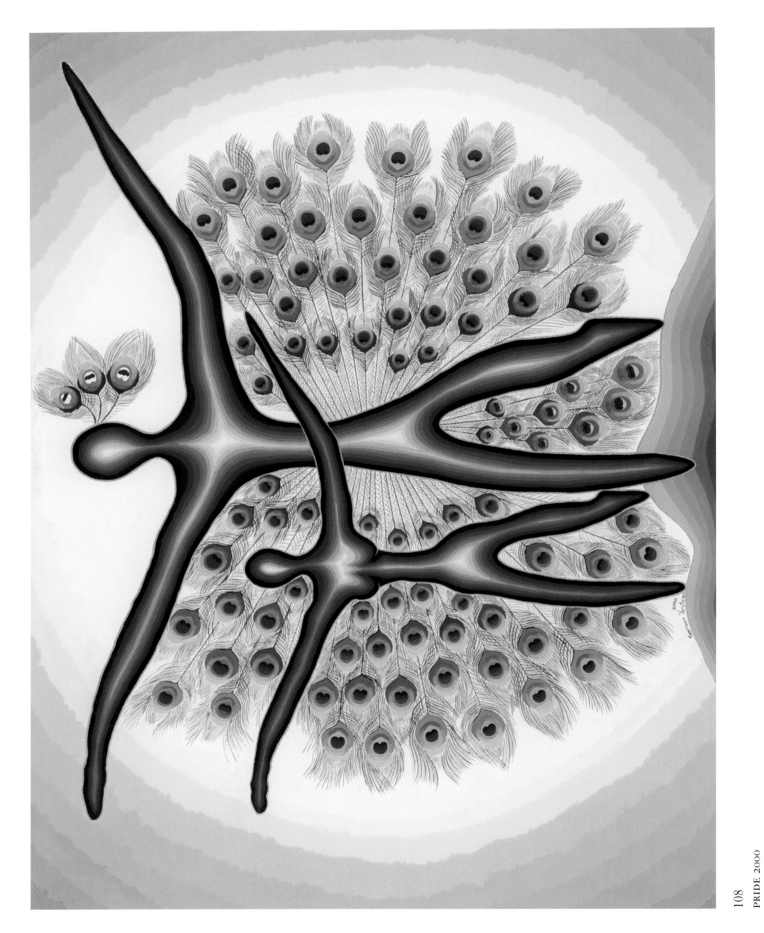

148

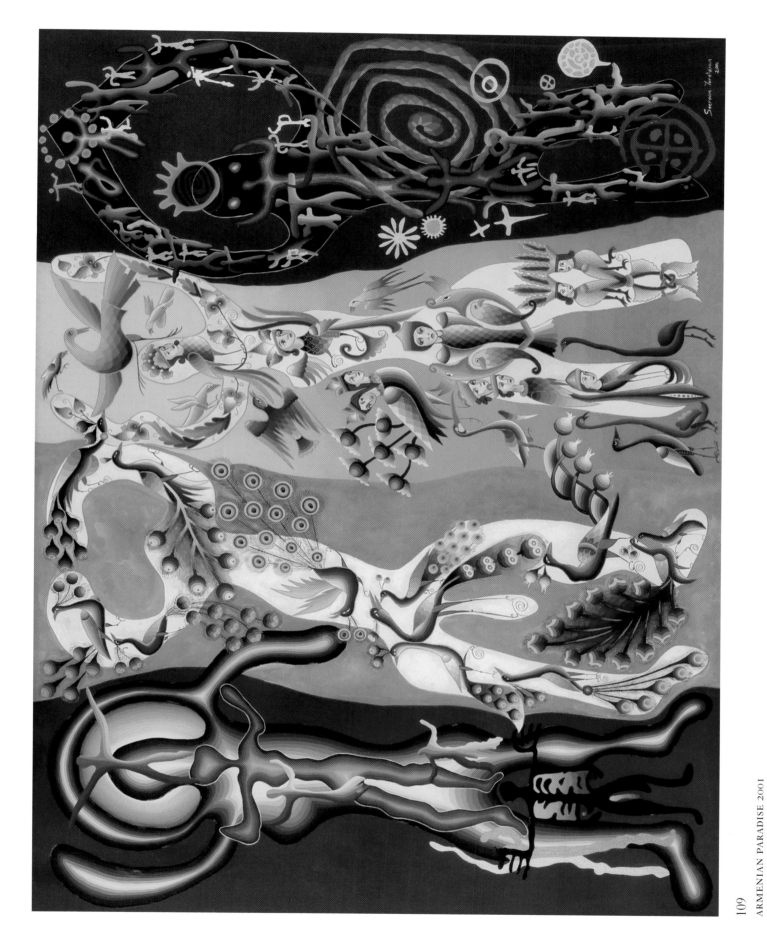

ARMENIAN PARADISE 2001

A bird doesn't sing because it has an answer,
it sings because it has a song.

MAYA ANGELOU

110
WATCHFUL EYES 2010

111
HEAVENLY PEACOCKS 2004

112
ROYAL PEACOCKS 2004

Seeron Yeretzian 1997

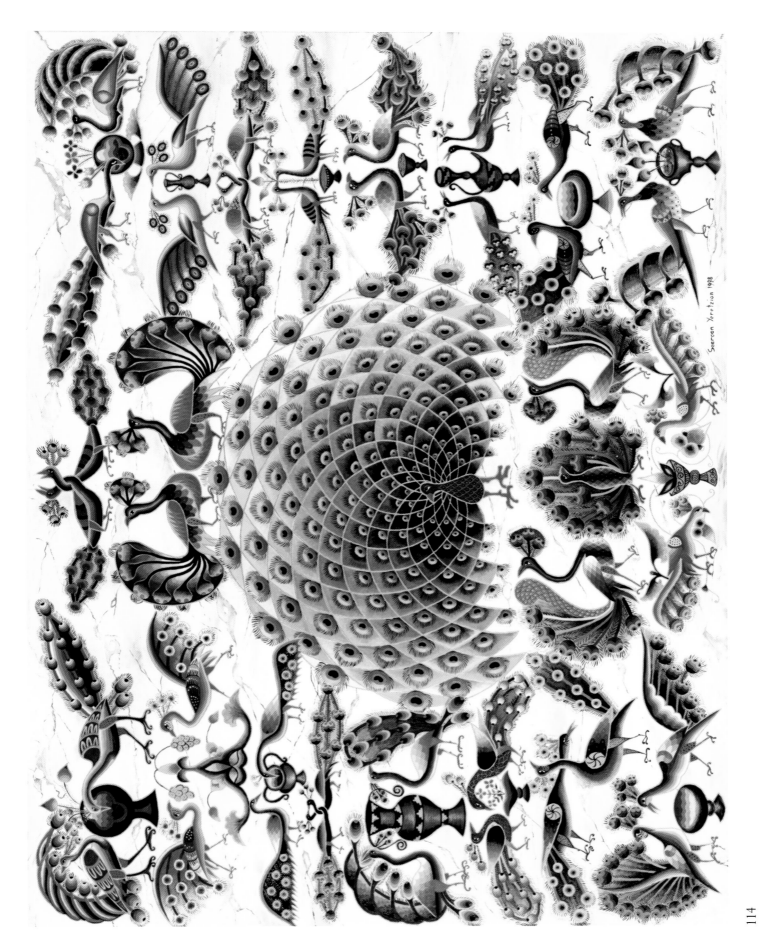

GARDEN OF PEACOCKS 1998

115
ENCHANTED PEACOCKS 2007

116
ARNO ILLUMINATED 2007

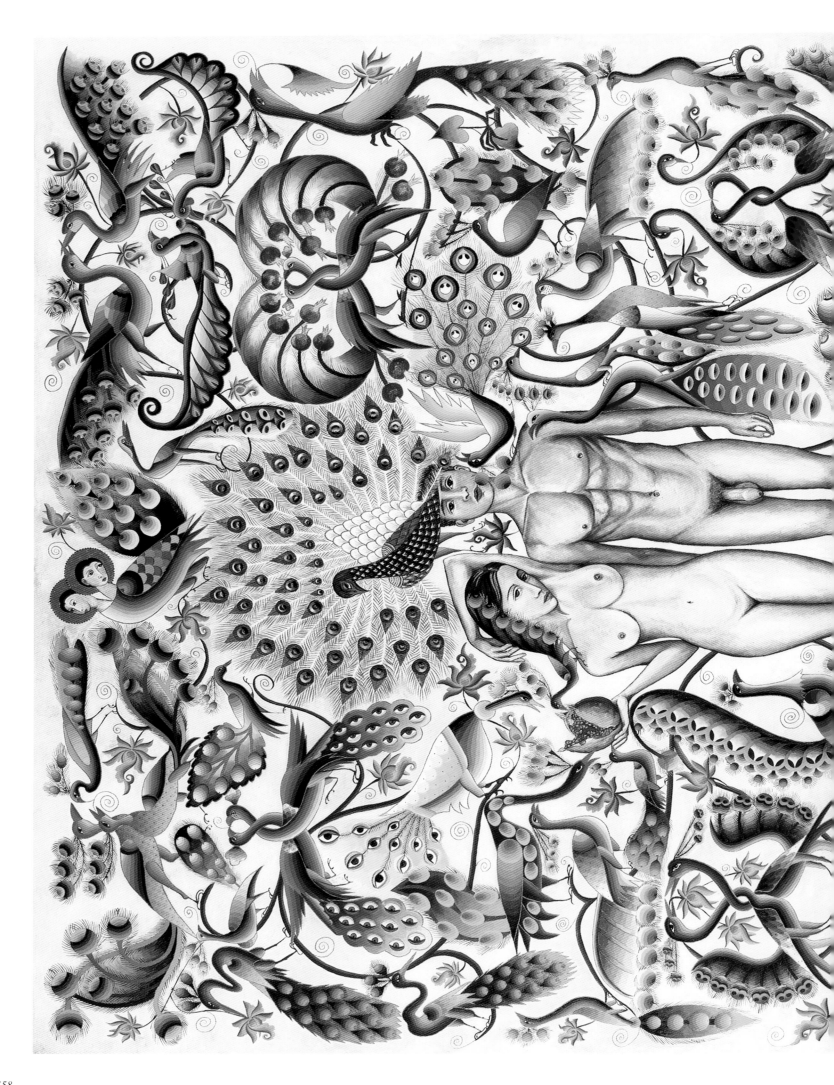

LOVERS AND PEACOCKS 2005

118
HOUSHGABARIGS 1998

119
GARDEN OF DELIGHTS 2011

120
NOYAN DABAN 1997

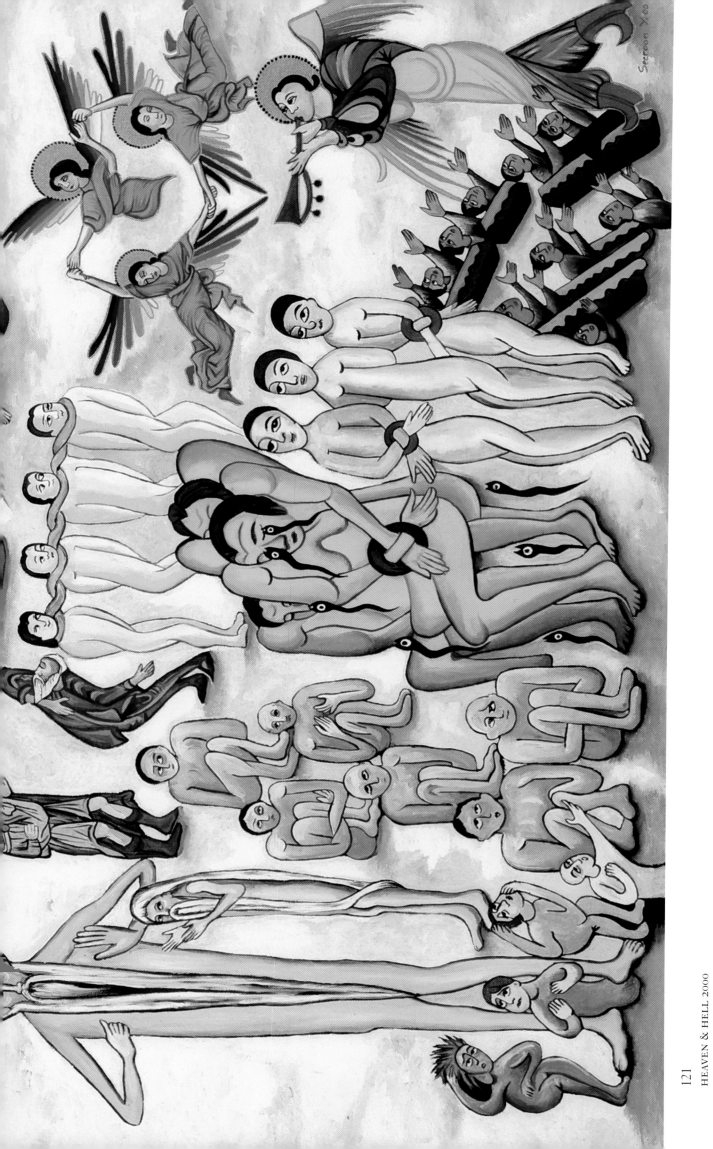

167

122

123

124

The Ornate Initials became my uncurable addiction,
  my happiness, my medication and meditation, my discipline
  and medium of patience. They serve as reservoirs of treasures,
  inherited from my ancestors, elevating me into a transcendental
state in the mechanical world of the 21st century.

SEEROON YERETZIAN

127

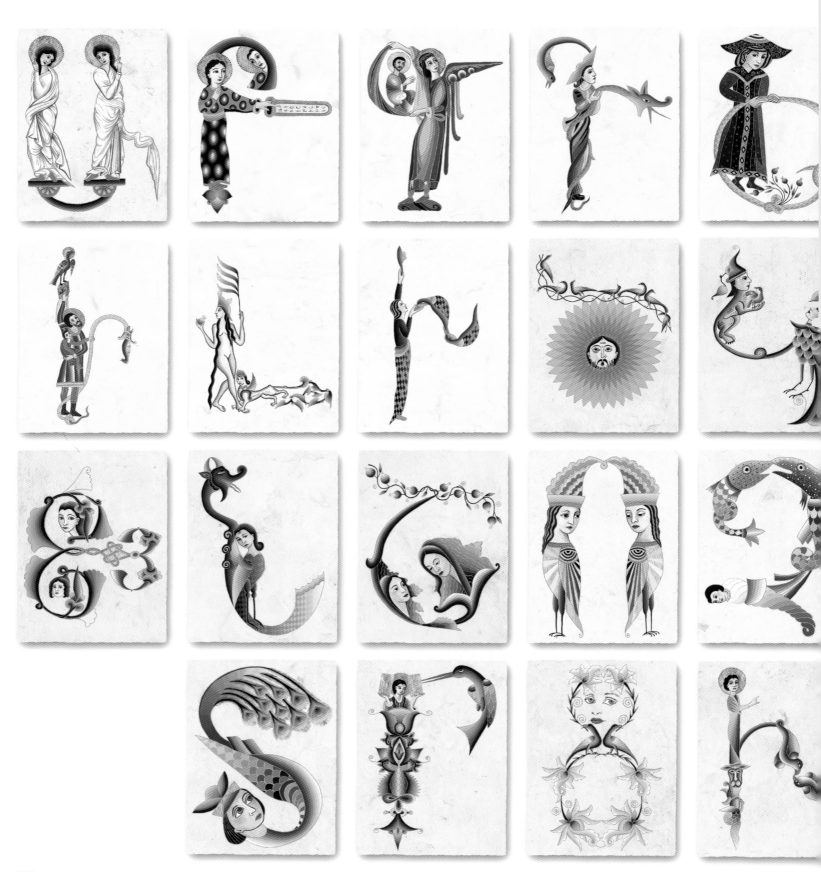

129

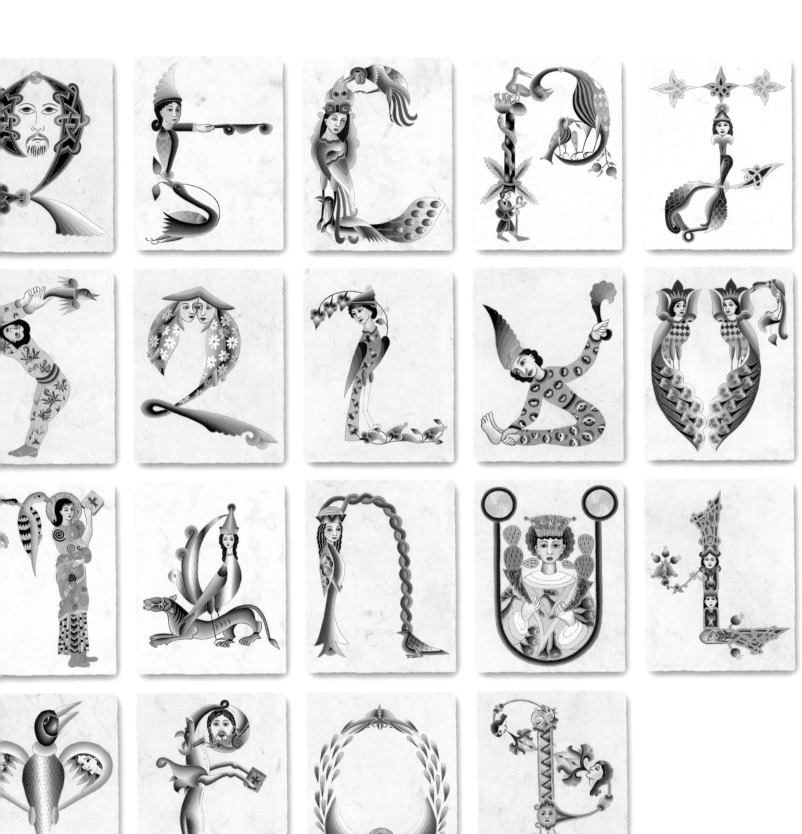

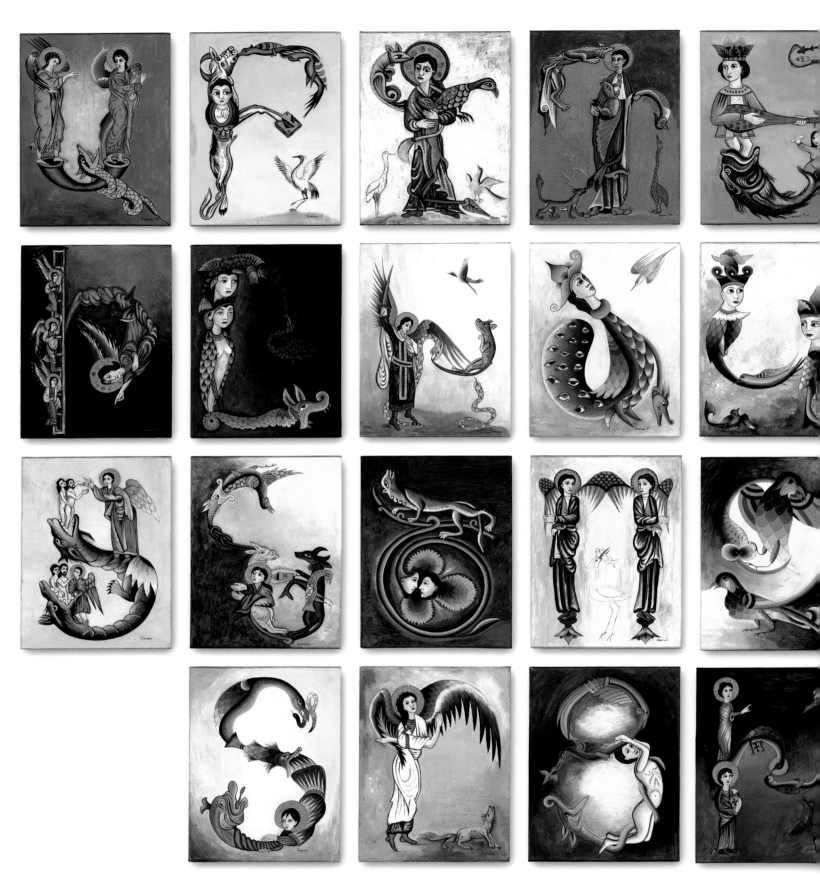

130

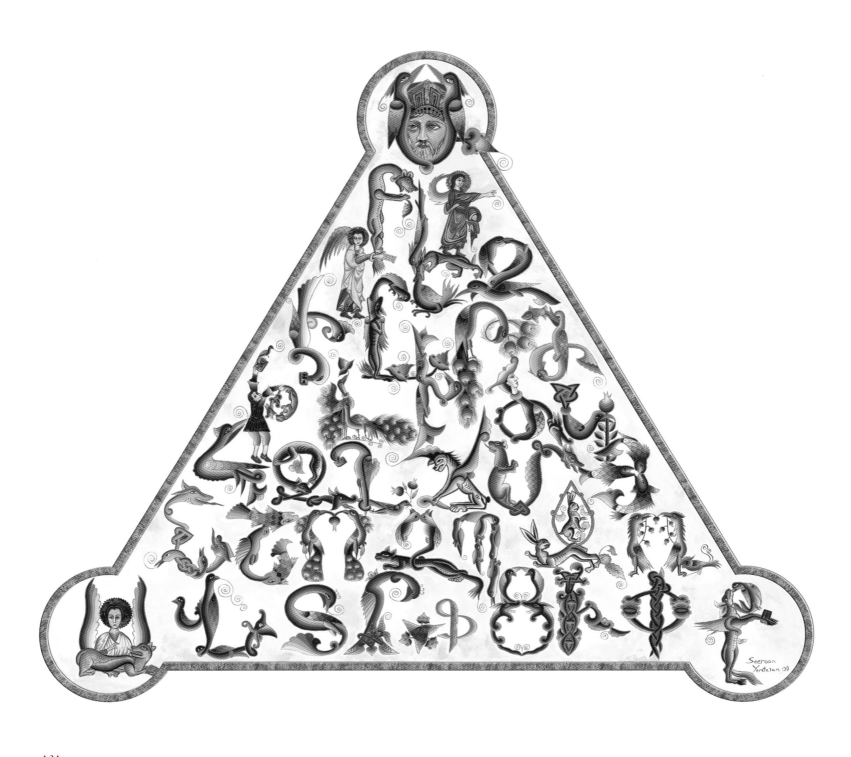

131
HOLY TRINITY 2009

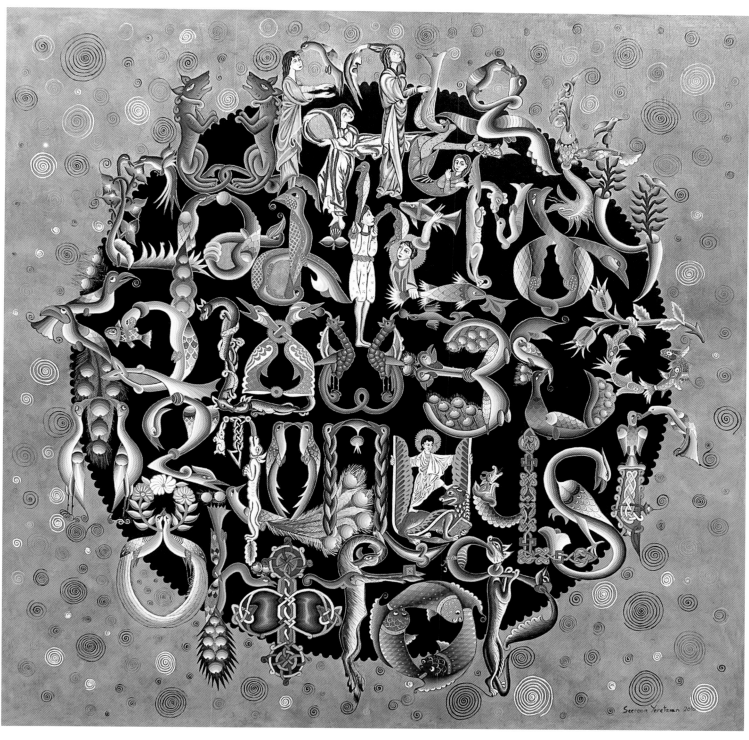

132
GOLDEN AYPUPEN 2010

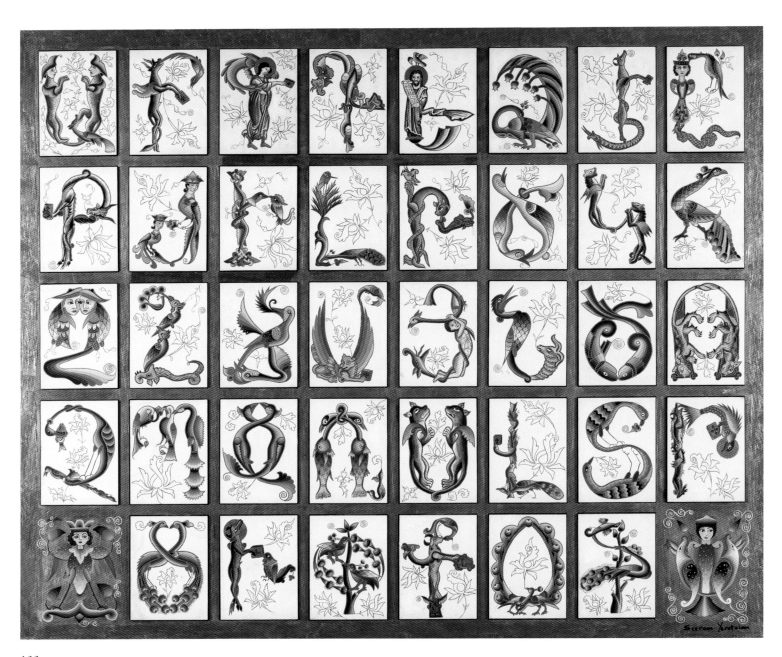

133
MESROBIAN AYPUPEN ????

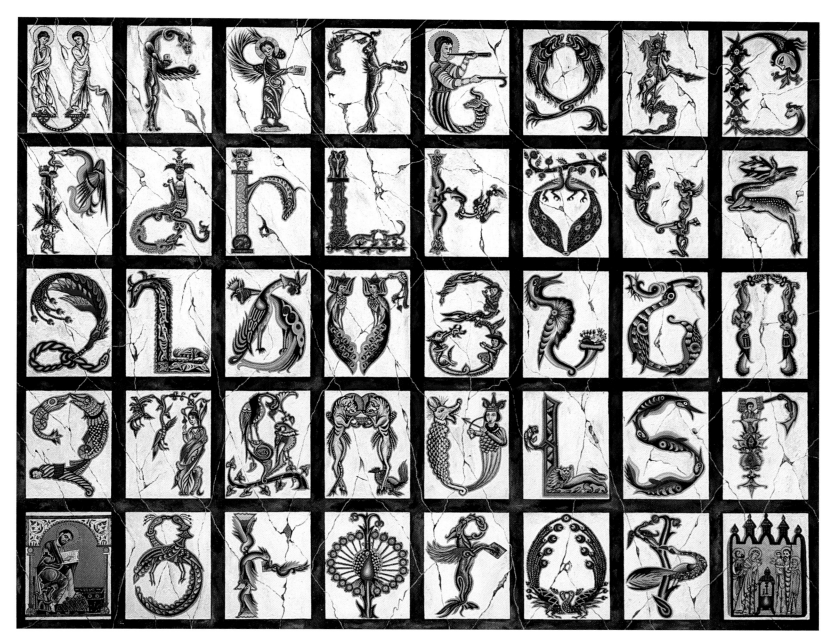

134

135

TRCHNAKEER AYPUPEN 2010

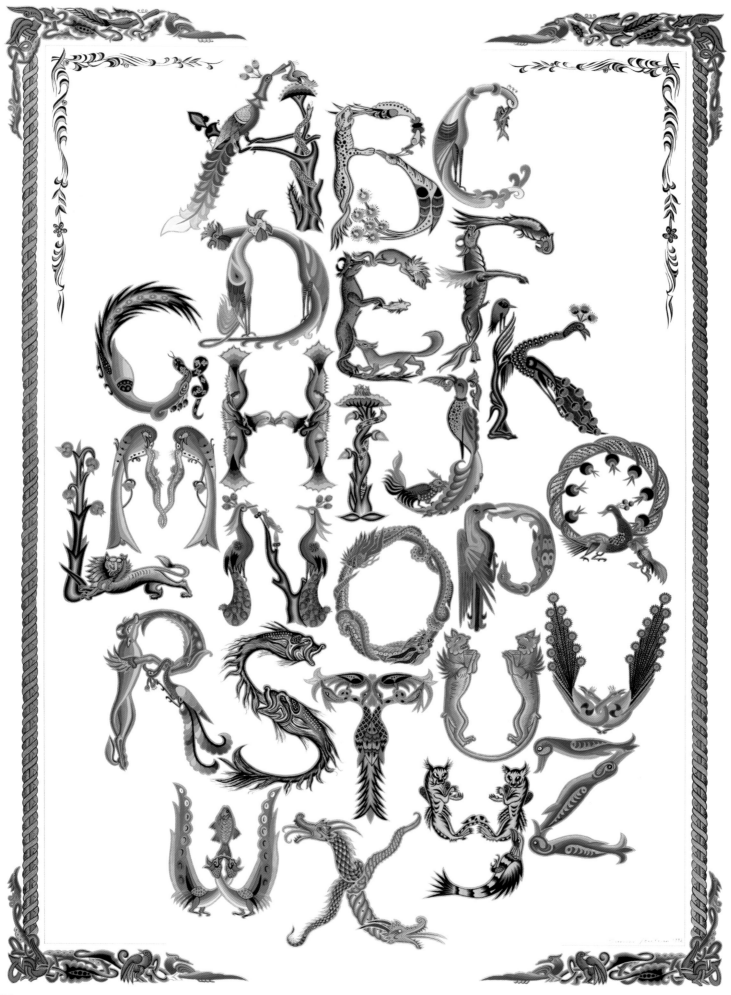

136
LATIN ALPHABET 1992

Seeroon Yeretzian (nee Siroun D. Vassilian) is born in 1951. She is the second child of five born to Dikran and Berjouhi in Beirut, Lebanon. Her siblings are Dikranouhie, Ani, Sona and Berge. She attends Vahan Tekeyan Elementary School (1954-1962) and A.G.B.U. Tarouhi Hagopian High School (1962-1969). She continues her education at the Coservatoire du Liban studying music (1968-1972) and Beirut University College studying Fashion Design (1972-1974).

In 1970 she meets Harout Yeretzian and they wed in 1973. 1976 becomes an eventful year as they welcome the arrival of their son, Arno, and the family migrates to the United States.

Seeroon continues her education by enrolling in the Extension Courses in Fine Arts at U.C.L.A. (1979-1981) and then attends Otis/Parsons Art Institute and School of Design, and receives her Bachelors Degree in Fine Arts in 1985.

In 1995 she establishes Roslin Art Gallery in Glendale, California. The gallery, dedicated to promoting Armenian artists, is as she says, "a working gallery," where she can often be found painting or illustrating Armenian ornate initials.

1

2

3

4

5

1. *Sister Ani, father Dikran and Seeroon (age 3), Tiro Camp, Lebanon, 1954*

2. *World renowned composer Aram Khatchadourian and Seeroon (age 11) at Tekeyan Elementary School, Beirut, Lebanon, 1962*

3. *From left: Sister Dikranouhie, father Dikran, cousin Krikor, a neighbor, sister Ani, Seeroon (age 10), mother Berjouhi, brother Berge, sister Sona, Lebanon, 1961*

4. *Husband Harout, Seeroon and son Arno, Glendale, California 2002*

5. *Seeroon at Roslin Art Gallery, Glendale, California 1996*

SELECTED SOLO & GROUP EXHIBITIONS

2006
Southern California
Women's Caucus for Art
I-5 Gallery
"Primarily Red"
Los Angeles, California

2005
National Audubon Society
"LA Under the Stars"
Los Angeles, California

2005
Armenian General
Benevolent Union
"1600th Armenian Alphabet
Anniversary"
San Francisco, California

2003
Armenian General
Benevolent Union
Young Professionals
"Arvest 2003"
Los Angeles, California

2003
Natural History Museum
of Los Angeles
"Celebrate L.A."
Los Angeles, California

2002
Armenian General
Benevolent Union
Young Professionals
"Arvest 2002 - Showcase
for the Arts"
West Los Angeles, California

2002
Exploratorium
"Traits of Life"
San Francisco, California

2001
Los Angeles Citywide
Public Display of Angels
"Angel of the Century"
Los Angeles, California

2001
San Francisco Public Library
"New Main to New Millennium"
San Francisco, California

2001
Getty Museum
"Family Festival"
Los Angeles, California

2001
Brand Library
"Modern Icon"
Glendale, California

2001
Laguna Niguel 4th Annual
Juried Show
"Echos & Visions IV"
Mission Viejo, California

2000
Modern Museum of Armenia
"Requiem to Genocide"
Yerevan, Armenia

2000
Brand Library
"Brand 30"
Glendale, California

2000
The Second City Council
"Beliefs, Faith & Religion"
Long Beach, California

2000
San Bernardino County Museum
"Inland Exhibition XXXVI"
San Bernardino, California

2000
Long Beach Art
"Figurative Art"
Long Beach, California

1999
William Still Grants Center
"Millennium Exhibition"
Los Angeles, California

1998
Downey Museum of Art
"Reflections '98"
Downey, California

1998
AGBU Alex Manoogian Center
Pasadena, California

1997
A.F.F.M.A.
"Women Artists"
Hollywood, California

1996
The Corridor Gallery of Art
"Immigrant Isle Group Show"
Hollywood, California

1996
St. John's Armenian Church
Cultural Hall
Southfield, Michigan

1996
J. Paul Getty Museum
"Book Arts of Isfahan"
Malibu, California

1993
Krikorian Headquarters
"Armenian Artists In Glendale"
Glendale, California

1991
Barakat Gallery
Beverly Hills, California

1991
Beshgeuturian Art Gallery
Altadena, California

1990
Shahbazian Residence
"Armenian Women In Art"
Santa Ana, California

1990
UCLA Kerchoff Art Gallery
Los Angeles, California

1989
Avedissian Hall
"Homage to
Armenian Women"
Encino, California

1988
UCLA Kerchoff Art Gallery
Los Angeles, CA

1988
Wilshire Ebell
Los Angeles, CA

1987
Armenian Society of Los Angeles
Los Angeles, California

1985
OTIS/Parsons Art Gallery
Los Angeles, California

1983
OTIS/Parsons Art Gallery
Los Angeles, California

Photo journal

With artist Puzant Godjamanian, Pasadena, California

With artist Jirair Zorthian, Los Angeles, California

From left to right: artist Jirair Zorthian (back turned), George Mandossian, Seeroon and artist Hagop Hagopian

With artist Joseph Giraco, Pasadena, California

With artist Garen Smbatyan, Pasadena, California

Arno, Seeroon and artist Grigor Khandjian, Yerevan, Armenian

With artist Jean Kazanjian and Harout Yeretzian

With Harout Yeretzian, stage director/caricaturist Vartan Ajemyan, Beirut, Lebanon

Photo journal

With artist Robert Elibekian, Baalbek, Lebanon

With artist Robert Elibekian and cinematographer Ruben Gevorgiantz

With Harout Yeretzian, artist Robert Elibekian and artist Osheen Kirkyasharian, Beirut, Lebanon

With artist Razmig Samvelts

With Harry Mesrobian and artist Vasken Matyan

With sculptor Varoujan Mardirian and Harout Yeretzian

Seroon and school colleague artist Patssi Valdez

With artist Aram Vartanov

With artists Natasha Kostan, Anne-Marie Chaglassian, Arlene Cartozian, Eileen Shahbazian, Ani Kupelian

Photo journal

With Harout Yeretzian and writer Sero Khanzadyan

With poet laurette Silva Gaboudigyan and Harout Yeretzian

With philanthropist Alex Manoogian and Fr. Baret Yeretzian

With Sona Hamalian and historian Professor Richard Hovannessian

From left to right, artist Eduard Issapekyan, Harout Yeretzian, Hovsep Fidanian, artist Seta Manougian and Seeroon

With writer/activist Zori Balayan
Pencil drawing of historian/diplomat John Guiragossian

From left to right: actor/editor Lutfi Tabakian, Varoujan Panossian, Seeeroon, Kima Panossian, writer Razmig Davoyan, Harout Yeretzian, writer Antranig Antreassian, composer Sassoon Paskevichyan, reciter Khatchig Araradian.

With artists/writer/actor/ Vahe Berberian at Abril Bookstore, Glendale, California

With Armenian Veterans of World War II, Etchmiadzin, Armenia

LIST OF PLATES

1

I EXIST 2010
oil on canvas
48 × 48 in. 121.92 × 121.92 cm.

2

BLOOMING 1988
oil on canvas
24 × 17 in. 60.96 × 43.18 cm.
Hovsep Tokat

3

THE ACADEMY 1985
oil on canvas
84 × 66 in. 213.36 × 167.6 cm.

4

ROSE BUDS 1988
oil on canvas
24 × 17 in. 60.96 × 43.18 cm.
Arpiar and Hermine Janoyan

5

THE WARLORD 1985
acrylic on canvas
84 × 66 in. 213.36 × 167.64 cm.

6

EVOLUTION 1998
oil on canvas
40 × 60 in. 101.6 × 152.4 cm.
Zaven Ghezelashouri

7

DISPOSABLE 1982
oil on canvas
40 × 60 in. 101.6 × 152.4 cm.
Barakat Gallery
Beverly Hills, California

8

EXPRESSIONS 1982
oil on canvas
40 × 48 in. 101.6 × 121.92 cm.

9

THE CHORUS 1987
oil on canvas
54 × 40 in. 137.16 × 101.6 cm.

10

MASKS 2008
oil on wood
54 × 30 in. 137.16 × 76.2 cm.

11

THE ECHO 1983
acrylic on canvas
36 × 24 in. 91.44 × 60.96 cm.

12

SCREAMERS 1982
oil on canvas
36 × 14 in. 91.44 × 35.56 cm.
Marine Panossian

13

HOMAGE TO H.B. I 1988
oil on canvas
48 × 24 in. 121.92 × 60.96 cm.
Manoogian Museum
Southfield, Michigan

14

HOMAGE TO H.B. II 1988
gouache on paper
30 × 22 in. 76.2 × 55.88 cm.
Tcherkezian Family

15

HOMAGE TO H.B. III 1988
gouache on paper
32 × 22 in. 81.28 × 55.88 cm.
Private Collection

16

CONDEMNED 1988
oil on wood
32 × 48 in. 81.28 × 121.92 cm.

17

BLOSSOMS ERUPT 2008
oil on canvas
36 × 36 in. 91.44 × 91.44 cm.

18

SON OF MAN 2008
oil on canvas mounted
on barbed wire wood frame
14 × 11 in. 35.56 × 27.94 cm.

19

SONS & DAUGHTERS 2008
oil on canvas mounted
on barbed wire wood frame
24 × 20 in. 60.96 × 50.8 cm.

20
SEAGULLS 2008
oil on canvas mounted
on barbed wire wood frame
20 × 16 in. 50.8 × 40.64 cm.

21
EYES OF INFINITY 2008
oil on canvas mounted
on barbed wire wood frame
24 × 20 in. 60.96 × 50.8 cm.

22
TRINITY 2009
acrylic on canvas
30 × 30 in. 76.2 × 76.2 cm.

23
HOMAGE FROM A TO Z 2005
oil on canvas
30 × 24 in. 76.2 × 60.96 cm.

24
HIS HOME 1989
gouache on board
24 × 20 in. 60.96 × 50.8 cm.
Sirvart Yeretzian

25
THE MATTRESS 1983
oil on canvas
36 × 48 in. 91.44 × 121.92 cm.

26
VANITY 1989
oil on canvas
36 × 48 in. 91.44 × 121.92 cm.
*Manoogian Museum
Detroit, Michigan*

27
DISCARDED 1999
oil on canvas
36 × 36 in. 91.44 × 91.44 cm.

28
SHOWCASE V 1992
oil on canvas
36 × 36 in. 91.44 × 91.44 cm.

29
TIME 1999
oil on canvas
24 × 30 in. 60.96 × 76.2 cm.

30
TIMELESS 1999
oil on canvas
30 × 32 in. 76.2 × 81.28 cm.

31
THE WASTE 1989
oil on canvas
36 × 36 in. 91.44 × 91.44 cm.
Sona Hamalian

32
THE BEGGARS 1989
oil on canvas
36 × 36 in. 91.44 × 91.44 cm.
Patricia Palacino

33
A DAY IN L.A. (TRIPTYCH) 1997
oil on canvas
60 × 148 in. 152.4 × 375.92 cm.

34
THE UNSPOKEN 1982
oil on canvas board
18 × 14 in. 45.72 × 35.56 cm.

35
HOME SWEET HOME I 1983
oil on canvas
54 × 40 in. 137.16 × 101.6 cm.
Sona Hamalian

36
SCRAPE 1990
acrylic on burlap
22 × 22 in. 55.88 × 55.88 cm.
Lutfi and Madlen Tabakian

37
PRAYER 1989
oil on canvas
54 × 48 in. 137.16 × 121.92 cm.

38
REMORSE 1990
oil on canvas
76 × 54 in. 193.04 × 137.16 cm.

39
THE TRAP 1990
oil on canvas
82 × 68 in. 208.28 × 172.72 cm.

40
SOLITUDE 1992
oil on canvas
24 × 20 in. 60.96 × 50.8 cm.
Harry Mesrobian

41
A PAGE IN LIFE 1991
oil on canvas
48 × 36 in. 121.92 × 91.44 cm.

42
THE THREE GRACES I 1992
oil on canvas
36 × 28 in. 91.44 × 71.12 cm.

43
ART OBJECTS 1992
oil on canvas
72 × 58 in. 182.88 × 147.32 cm.

44
THE WOMB 1994
oil on paper
30 × 22 in. 76.2 × 55.88 cm.
Private Collection

45
ADAM & EVE 1994
oil on canvas
77 × 57 in. 195.58 × 144.78 cm.

46
REFLECTION 1993
oil on canvas
36 × 24 in. 91.44 × 60.96 cm.
Seta Kassabian

47
QUO VADIS 1994
oil on canvas
48 × 30 in. 121.92 × 76.2 cm.

48
TRANSPOSED 1994
oil on paper
30 × 22 in. 76.2 × 55.88 cm.
Hovik Abrahamyan

49
VENI, VIDI 1994
oil on canvas
48 × 30 in. 121.92 × 76.2 cm.

50
ETERNITY 1990
gouache on paper
40 × 30 in. 101.6 × 76.2 cm.

51
FREEDOM 1993
acrylic on canvas
36 × 24 in. 91.44 × 60.96 cm.
Norma Bardakjian

52
FORGIVENESS 1990
oil on canvas
68 × 60 in. 172.72 × 152.4 cm.

53
UNCERTAINTY I 1989
gouache on paper
22 × 30 in. 55.88 × 76.2 cm.
Vahan and Maral Voskian

54
UNCERTAINTY IV 1993
oil on canvas
34 × 24 in. 86.36 × 60.96 cm.

55
THE THREE GRACES II 1992
oil on canvas
36 × 36 in. 91.44 × 91.44 cm.
Vahan and Maral Voskian

56
NATURE CRUCIFIED 2006
acrylic and oil on wood
48 × 34 in. 121.92 × 86.36 cm.

57
FREEDOM II 1993
oil on canvas board
18 × 12 in. 45.72 × 30.48 cm.
Edmond and Holly Mesrobian

58
SUBMISSION 1990
oil on paper
40 × 30 in. 101.6 × 76.2 cm.
Joseph Kanimian

59
AUTO PORTRAIT 1980-2005
oil on canvas
36 × 36 in. 91.44 × 91.44 cm.

60
DEATH & LIFE (DIPTYCH) 1984
oil on canvas
54 × 132 in. 137.16 × 335.28 cm.

61
MY JOURNEY I 1990
oil on canvas
48 × 48 in. 121.92 × 121.92 cm.

62
SOUL TO SOLE 2009
oil on canvas
30 × 40 in. 76.2 × 101.6 cm.

63
BEARER OF LOVE 2009
oil on board
26 × 33 in. 66.04 × 83.82 cm.

64
DAY & NIGHT 1995
oil on canvas
48 × 36 in. 121.92 × 91.44 cm.

65
MADONNA III 1994
oil on canvas
40 × 30 in. 101.6 × 76.2 cm.

66
MADONNA I 1994
oil on canvas
48 × 30 in. 121.92 × 76.2 cm.

67
MEDITATION 1997
oil on canvas
50 × 36 in. 127 × 91.44 cm.

68
BRIGITTE 1994
oil on canvas
48 × 22 in. 121.92 × 55.88 cm.

69
MOTHER EARTH 1993
oil on wood
167.64 × 81.28 cm. 66 × 32 in.

70
VENUS TRAPPED 2009
oil on canvas
80 × 32 in. 203.2 × 81.28 cm.

71
EMPTY NEST 1993
acrylic on canvas
36 × 24 in. 91.44 × 60.96 cm.

72
ENIGMA 1996
oil on canvas and burlap
46 × 36 in. 116.84 × 91.44 cm.

73
EVALUTION 2008
oil on canvas
48 × 36 in. 121.92 × 91.44 cm.
Zaven Ghezelashouri

74
HUMANIMALS 2008
oil on canvas
48 × 36 in. 121.92 × 91.44 cm.

75
MONSTRE SACRE II 1994
oil on canvas
35 × 22 in. 88.9 × 55.88 cm.

76
INTROSPECTION 1997
oil on canvas
28 × 22 in. 71.12 × 55.88 cm.

77
SUPER WO-MAN 1999
mixed media on arches paper
30 × 22 in. 76.2 × 55.88 cm.

78
MAN AT DAWN II 2000
mixed media on paper
22 × 30 in. 55.88 × 76.2 cm.

79
CHAINS OF TIME 2003
oil on canvas
40 × 30 in. 101.6 × 76.2 cm.

80
PAST & PRESENT 2003
oil on canvas
40 × 30 in. 101.6 × 76.2 cm.

81
TRAPPED FOREVER 2003
oil on canvas
40 × 30 in. 101.6 × 76.2 cm.

82
PRIMAL EYES 2003
oil on canvas
40 × 30 in. 101.6 × 76.2 cm.

83
HUMAN ARCHEOLOGY 2004
oil on canvas
36 × 24 in. 91.44 × 60.96 cm.

84
PHENOMENAL 2004
oil on canvas
36 × 24 in. 91.44 × 60.96 cm.

85
SANCTUARY 2004
oil on canvas
36 × 24 in. 91.44 × 60.96 cm.

86
ECLECTIC 2004
oil on canvas
36 × 24 in. 91.44 × 60.96 cm.

87
HIDDEN TREASURES 2004
oil on canvas
36 × 24 in. 91.44 × 60.96 cm.

88
UNVEILED 2004
oil on canvas
36 × 24 in. 91.44 × 60.96 cm.

89
MATRIARCHS 2001
mixed media on two boards
40 × 28 in. 101.6 × 71.12 cm.

90
THE OTHER SIDE 2004
oil on canvas
36 × 24 in. 91.44 × 60.96 cm.

91
CROWN IN WEB 1999
mixed media on
hand-made paper
30 × 22 in. 76.2 × 55.88 cm.

92
LAND & SEA 2000
mixed media on arches paper
30 × 22 in. 76.2 × 55.88 cm.
Ara Babayan

93
HONEYCOMB I 1999
mixed media on arches paper
30 × 22 in. 76.2 × 55.88 cm.
Guiragos Minassian

94
WISH 2000
mixed media on arches paper
29 × 22 in. 73.66 × 55.88 cm.

95
GIANTS AND MIDGETS 2001
mixed media on board
40 × 32 in. 101.6 × 81.28 cm.

96
ECSTASY 2000
mixed media on arches paper
30 × 23 in. 76.2 × 58.42 cm.

97
TRACES 1999
mixed media on arches paper
30 × 23 in. 76.2 × 58.42 cm.

98
DANCE OF TIME 2000
mixed media on arches paper
23 × 30 in. 58.4 × 76.2 cm.

99
FRAMED FOREVER 2000
mixed media on arches paper
23 × 30 in. 58.42 × 76.2 cm.

100
PETRIFIED CIVILIZATION 1998
mixed media on board
28 × 40 in. 71.12 × 101.6 cm.

101
ENFANTS PERDU 1999
mixed media on
hand-made paper
24.5 × 36 in. 62.23 × 91.44 cm.

102
WRAPPED AROUND 2000
mixed media on
hand-made paper
31 × 21 in. 78.74 × 53.34 cm.

103
COSMIC UNITY 2000
mixed media on arches paper
30 × 22 in. 76.2 × 55.88 cm.

104
ENTRAPPED I 2000
mixed media on arches paper
30 × 22 in. 76.2 × 55.88 cm.

105
TORNADO 1999
mixed media on
hand-made paper
30 × 22 in. 76.2 × 55.88 cm.
Vahan and Maral Voskian

106
ATLAS 1999
mixed media on
hand-made paper
30 × 22 in. 76.2 × 55.88 cm.

107
GODDESS 1999
mixed media on
hand-made paper
30 × 22 in. 76.2 × 55.88 cm.
Antranik and Flora Mesrobian

108
PRIDE 2000
mixed media on arches paper
30 × 22 in. 76.2 × 55.88 cm.

109
ARMENIAN PARADISE 2001
mixed media on board
29 × 39 in. 73.66 × 99.06 cm.

110
WATCHFUL EYES 2010
oil on canvas
48 × 48 in. 121.92 × 121.92 cm.

111
HEAVENLY PEACOCKS 2004
oil on canvas
54 × 54 in. 137.16 × 137.16 cm.
Manoogian Museum
Southfield, Michigan

112
ROYAL PEACOCKS 2004
oil on canvas
30 × 36 in. 76.2 × 91.44 cm.
Osep and Dr. Nadia Sarafian

113
SEERAMARKS 1997
oil on canvas
32 × 40 in. 81.28 × 101.6 cm.
Private Collection

114
GARDEN OF PEACOCKS 1998
oil on canvas
32 × 40 in. 81.28 × 101.6 cm.
Private Collection

115
ENCHANTED PEACOCKS 2007
oil on canvas
31 × 36 in. 78.74 × 91.44 cm.

116
ARNO ILLUMINATED 2007
oil on canvas
60 × 48 in. 152.4 × 121.92 cm.

117
LOVERS AND PEACOCKS 2005
oil on canvas
60 × 48 in. 152.4 × 121.92 cm.

118
HOUSHGABARIGS 1998
oil on canvas
30 × 60 in. 76.2 × 152.4 cm.
Zaven Ghezelashouri

119
GARDEN OF DELIGHTS 2011
oil on canvas
36 × 60 in. 91.44 × 152.4 cm.

120
NOYAN DABAN 1997
oil on canvas
30 × 44 in. 76.2 × 111.76 cm.

121
HEAVEN & HELL 2000
oil on canvas
48 × 36 in. 121.92 × 91.44 cm.

122
SPRING 2005
oil on canvas
48 × 48 in. 121.92 × 121.92 cm.

123
SUMMER 2005
oil on canvas
48 × 48 in. 121.92 × 121.92 cm.

124
AUTUMN 2005
oil on canvas
48 × 48 in. 121.92 × 121.92 cm.

125
WINTER 2005
oil on canvas
48 × 48 in. 121.92 × 121.92 cm.

126
SPLENDOR OF AYPUPEN 1989
gouache on illustration board
39 × 27 in. 99.06 × 68.58 cm.
Vahan and Maral Voskian

127
GLORY OF AYPUPEN 2003
oil on canvas
60 × 48 in. 152.4 × 121.92 cm.

128
SEEROON AYPUPEN 2003
oil on canvas
60 × 48 in. 152.4 × 121.92 cm.

129
ELEGANT AYPUPEN 2009
gouache on parchment paper,
38 individual pieces
15 × 11 in. 38.1 × 27.94 cm.

130
MARVELOUS AYPUPEN 2009
oil on canvas,
38 individual pieces
16 × 12 in. 40.64 × 30.48 cm.

131
HOLY TRINITY 2009
gouache on illustration board
34 × 34 × 34 in. 86.36 × 86.36 × 86.36 cm.
Vatche and Arpy Mankerian

132
GOLDEN AYPUPEN 2010
oil on canvas
48 × 48 in. 121.92 × 121.92 cm.
Edmond and Holly Mesrobian

133
MESROBIAN AYPUPEN 1996
oil on clay tablets,
mounted on wood
41 × 48 in. 104.14 × 121.92 cm.
Harry Mesrobian

134
BEAUTIFUL AYPUPEN 1993
oil on canvas
48 × 60 in. 121.92 × 152.4 cm.
Richard Manoogian Collection

135
TRCHNAKEER AYPUPEN 2010
oil on canvas
48 × 36 in. 121.92 × 91.44 cm.

136
LATIN ALPHABET 1992
gouache on board
36 × 25 in. 91.44 × 63.5 cm.
Mardigian Library
Detroit, Michigan

END-SHEET PLATES

1. COMME DE GARCONNES VI 1994
acrylic on material
60 × 34 in. 152.4 × 86.36 cm.
Dr. Ara Poladian

2. QUAI D'ORSAY 1994
oil on canvas board
18 × 24 in. 45.72 × 60.96 cm.

3. SHOWCASE II 1995
oil on canvas
30 × 24 in. 76.2 × 60.96 cm.
Vahan Saroyantz

4. NUDE FEMALE NO. 32 1992
acrylic on board
15 × 20 in. 30.1 × 50.8 cm.
Arpi Sarafian

5. COMME DE GARCONNES VIII 1990
oil on board
30 × 20 in. 76.2 × 50.8 cm.
Fr. Baret Yeretzian

6. NUDE FEMALE NO. 30 1982
oil on board
24 × 16 in. 60.96 × 40.64 cm.
Varoujan Mardirian

7. NUDE FEMALE NO. 35 1982
acrylic on board
18 × 23 in. 45.72 × 58.42 cm.

8. PRIVATE PROPERTY II 1994
oil on canvas
48 × 36 in. 121.92 × 91.44 cm.
Lucy Sarkisian

9. COMME DES GARCONNES X 1990
oil on board
24 × 18 in. 60.96 × 45.72 cm.
Joseph Kanimian

10. MONSTRE SACRE I 1994
oil on canvas
39 × 16 in. 99.06 × 40.64 cm.
Hagop Boghossian

11. THE ETERNAL DANCE II 1993
oil on wood
30 × 40 in. 76.2 × 101.6 cm.
Armen Harutunian

12. HAROUT YERETZIAN I 1983
oil on canvas
24 × 18 in. 60.96 × 45.72 cm.

13. SHOWCASE I 1992
mixed media on paper
10 × 8 in. 25.4 × 20.32 cm.
Souren and Sona Derstepanian

14. DES CHOSES DE LA VIE 1991
gouache on board
28 × 20 in. 71.12 × 50.8 cm.
Souren and Sona Derstepanian

15. SISTERS III 1987
oil on canvas board
16 × 24 in. 40.64 × 60.96 cm.
Private Collection

16. SISTERS I 1987
oil on canvas
24 × 16 in. 60.96 × 40.64 cm.
Private Collection

17. WATCHFUL EYES I 2006
oil on wood
30 × 16 in. 76.2 × 40.64 cm.
Nune Simonian

18. SHOWCASE I 1992
mixed media on paper
18 × 24 in. 45.72 × 60.96 cm.
Nercess and Sossi Yeretzian

19. ARMEN MANASSERIAN 2008
oil on canvas
20 × 16 in. 50.8 × 40.64 cm.
Nune Simonian

20. SELF PORTRAIT -
A LA VAN GOGH 1981
oil on paper
30 × 22 in. 76.2 × 55.88 cm.

21. TENDER LOVE 2006
oil and material on wood
24 × 24 in. 60.96 × 60.96 cm.
Private Collection

22. THE HUMAN JUNGLE 1994
oil on canvas
34 × 41 in. 86.36 × 104.14 cm.
Mardiros Iskenderian

23. UNCERTAINTY II 1990
mixed media on board
24 × 18 in. 60.96 × 45.72 cm.
Vatche and Sossy Semerdjian

24. VATCHE SEMERDJIAN I 1986
acrylic on canvas
36 × 22 in. 91.44 × 55.88 cm.
Vatche and Sossy Semerdjian

25. OLD FASHION 1993
pastel on hand paper
16 × 24 in. 40.64 × 60.96 cm.
Jesse and Silvia Matossian

26. ENTRY INTO JERUSALEM 1997
oil on leather
36 × 28 in. 91.44 × 71.12 cm.
Ashkhen Mouradian

27. ARMENIAN WEDDING 1990
oil on canvas
48 × 48 in. 121.92 × 121.92 cm.

28. NURSING YOUNG GIRL 1993
pastel on paper
16 × 12 in. 40.64 × 30.48 cm.
Dickran and Melo Ekizian

29. REFUGEES 1993
pastel on paper
16 × 12 in. 40.64 × 30.48 cm.
Private Collection

30. THE WINDOW 1994
oil on canvas
48 × 30 in. 121.92 × 76.2 cm.
Varteres Karageuzian

31. FLIGHT 1993
acrylic on board
28 × 20 in. 71.12 × 50.8 cm.
Shavarsh and Maria Chrissian

32. IF I WAS IN ADANA 1990
oil on canvas
44 × 32 in. 111.76 × 81.28 cm.

33. FEDAYEES III 1993
pastel on paper
18 × 24 in. 45.72 × 60.96 cm.
Souren and Sona Derstepanian

34. FIRST STEPS I 1999
mixed media on
hand made paper
22 × 13 in. 55.88 × 33.02 cm.
Stepanouhi Uluhogian

35. DEFILEE 2000
mixed media on canvas
24 × 36 in. 60.96 × 91.44 cm.

36. ETERNAL ECSTASY 1989
gouache on arches paper
11 × 11 in. 27.94 × 27.94 cm.
Private Collection

37. STAR STEPS 1999
mixed media on
hand made paper
35 × 22 in. 88.90 × 55.88 cm.
Mark and Laura Bogner

38. DESTINY 1989
gouache on arches paper
11 × 11 in. 27.94 × 27.94 cm.
Private Collection

39. SUPERMAN 1989
gouache on arches paper
11 × 11 in. 27.94 × 27.94 cm.
Private Collection

40. THE PRINCE III 1999
acrylic on board
13 × 20 in. 33.02 × 50.8 cm.

41. WAVES 2000
mixed media on
hand made paper
31 × 22 in. 78.74 × 55.88 cm.

42. THE DEFEAT OF DEATH 1989
gouache on arches paper
11 × 11 in. 27.94 × 27.94 cm.
Private Collection

43. THE PRINCE I 1998
acrylic on board
20 × 13 in. 50.8 × 33.02 cm.
Arpiar and Rita Demirjian

44. PUZZLE 2000
mixed media on
hand made paper
30 × 22 in. 76.2 × 55.88 cm.
Private Collection

45. QUEEN BEE 2001
mixed media on board
33 × 19 in. 83.82 × 48.26 cm.
Tara Kotchounian

46. MERVEILLE 1999
mixed media on
hand made paper
27.5 × 19.5 in. 69.85 × 49.53 cm.
Nune Simonian

ACKNOWLEDGMENTS

I gratefully acknowledge the following people for being in my life and for their support on personal and/or artistic levels.

Harout Yeretzian

Arno Yeretzian

Harry Mesrobian

Souren and Sona Derstepanian

Vatche and Sossy Semerdjian

A most endearing thank you to the following individuals who have supported me throughout the years.

Edmond Azadian

Monique Gevorkian

Vatche Mankerian

Edmond and Holly Mesrobian

Nune Simonian

Vahan and Maral Voskian

A special thank you to the following individuals for their valuable contribution in the editing of this book.

Yervant Kotchounian

Jesse Matossian

Arpi Sarafian

Arno Yeretzian

PHOTOGRAPHIC CREDITS

Vatche Alexanian

Mher Vahakn

Arno Yeretzian

26

27

28

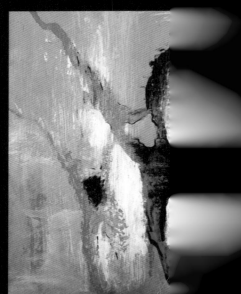

30

31

29